The Nation in Crisis
1861-1877

GOLDENTREE BIBLIOGRAPHIES

In American History

under the series editorship of

Arthur S. Link

The Nation in Crisis 1861-1877

compiled by

David Donald

The Johns Hopkins University

APPLETON-CENTURY CROFTS

Educational Division

New York MEREDITH CORPORATION

619–1

Library of Congress Card Number: 74-79169

PRINTED IN THE UNITED STATES OF AMERICA

390-27038-5

Editor's Foreword

GOLDENTREE BIBLIOGRAPHIES IN AMERICAN HISTORY are designed to provide students, teachers, and librarians with ready and reliable guides to the literature of American History in all its remarkable scope and variety. Volumes in the series cover comprehensively the major periods in American history, while additional volumes are devoted to all important subjects,

Goldentree Bibliographies attempt to steer a middle course between the brief list of references provided in the average textbook and the long bibliography in which significant items are often lost in the sheer number of titles listed. Each bibliography is, therefore, selective, with the sole criterion for choice being the significance—and not the age—of any particular work. The result is bibliographies of all works, including journal articles and doctoral dissertations, that are still useful, without bias in favor of any particular historiographical school.

Each compiler is a scholar long associated, both in research and teaching, with the period or subject of his volume. All compilers have not only striven to accomplish the objective of this series but have also cheerfully adhered to a general style and format. However, each compiler has been free to define his field, make his own selections, and work out internal organization as the unique demands of his period or subject have seemed to dictate.

The single great objective of *Goldentree Bibliographies in American History* will have been achieved if these volumes help researchers and students to find their way to the significant literature of American history.

Arthur S. Link

Abbreviations

A Lincoln Q	*Abraham Lincoln Quarterly*
Ag Hist	*Agricultural History*
Ala Rev	*Alabama Review*
Am Econ Rev	*American Economic Review*
Am Hist Rev	*American Historical Review*
Am Hist Assoc Ann Rep	*American Historical Association, Annual Report*
Am Jew Hist Soc Q	*American Jewish Historical Society Quarterly*
Am J Int Law	*American Journal of International Law*
Atl Mo	*Atlantic Monthly*
Buffalo Law Rev	*Buffalo Law Review*
Cath Hist Rev	*Catholic Historical Review*
Church Hist	*Church History*
Cincinnati Hist Soc Bull	*Cincinnati Historical Society Bulletin*
C W Hist	*Civil War History*
Col Law Rev	*Columbia Law Review*
E Tenn Hist Soc Pub	*East Tennessee Historical Society Publications*
Explorations in Entrepreneurial Hist	*Explorations in Entrepreneurial History*
Fla Hist Q	*Florida Historical Quarterly*
Ga Hist Q	*Georgia Historical Quarterly*
Har Law Rev	*Harvard Law Review*
His-Am Hist Rev	*Hispanic-American Historical Review*
Historian	*The Historian*
Hist	*History*
Hist Today	*History Today*
Ind Mag Hist	*Indiana Magazine of History*
Iowa J Hist and Pol	*Iowa Journal of History and Politics*
J Am Hist	*Journal of American History*
J Econ Hist	*Journal of Economic History*
J Hist Ideas	*Journal of the History of Ideas*
J Ill State Hist Soc	*Journal of the Illinois State Historical Society*
J Miss Hist	*Journal of Mississippi History*
J Neg Ed	*Journal of Negro Education*
J Neg Hist	*Journal of Negro History*
J Pol Econ	*Journal of Political Economy*
J S Hist	*Journal of Southern History*
La Hist Q	*Louisiana Historical Quarterly*
La Hist	*Louisiana History*
Md Hist Mag	*Maryland Historical Magazine*
Mich Law Rev	*Michigan Law Review*
Mich Q	*Michigan Quarterly*
Mich Q Rev	*Michigan Quarterly Review*

Mid-Am	*Mid-America*
Miss Val Hist Rev	*Mississippi Valley Historical Review*
Mo Hist Rev	*Missouri Historical Review*
Neg Hist Bull	*Negro History Bulletin*
N Eng Q	*New England Quarterly*
N Y Hist	*New York History*
N Y Univ Law Rev	*New York University Law Review*
Ohio Arch and Hist Q	*Ohio Archaeological and Historical Quarterly*
Ore Hist Q	*Oregon Historical Quarterly*
Pac Hist Rev	*Pacific Historical Review*
Pacific NW Hist Q	*Pacific Northwest Historical Quarterly*
Partisan Rev	*Partisan Review*
Past and Present	
Penn Mag Hist and Biog	*Pennsylvania Magazine of History and Biography*
Pol Sci Q	*Political Science Quarterly*
Proc Am Philos Soc	*Proceedings, American Philosophical Society*
Proc Leeds Phil Soc	*Proceedings, Leeds Philosophical Society*
Proc Mass Hist Soc	*Proceedings, Massachusetts Historical Society*
Pub Miss Hist Soc	*Publications of the Mississippi Historical Society*
Q J Econ	*Quarterly Journal of Economics*
Russian Rev	*Russian Review*
Sci and Soc	*Science and Society*
Slavic and E European Rev	*Slavic and Eastern European Review*
S Atl Q	*South Atlantic Quarterly*
S C Hist Mag	*South Carolina Historical Magazine*
Stanford Law Rev	*Stanford Law Review*
Sw Hist Q	*Southwestern Historical Quarterly*
Sw So Sci Q	*Southwestern Social Sciences Quarterly*
Susquehanna Univ Stud	*Susquehanna University Studies*
Tenn Hist Q	*Tennessee Historical Quarterly*
Topic	
Univ of Chicago Law Rev	*University of Chicago Law Review*
Vanderbilt Law Rev	*Vanderbilt Law Review*
Va Mag Hist & Biog	*Virginia Magazine of History & Biography*
W Va Hist	*West Virginia History*
W Pol Q	*Western Political Quarterly*
Wisc Law Rev	*Wisconsin Law Review*
Wisc Mag Hist	*Wisconsin Magazine of History*
Yale Law Rev	*Yale Law Review*

Note: Cross-references are to pages (**boldface**) and to item numbers (roman). Items marked by a dagger (†) are available in paperback edition at the time this bibliography goes to press. The publisher and compiler invite suggestions for additions to future editions of the bibliography.

Contents

I. Bibliographies and Other Guides to Further Study

1 ADAMS, James T., *et al.*, eds. *Dictionary of American History.* 6 vols. plus index. New York, 1940-1961. (Short articles, each by an expert, with brief bibliographies.)

2 BASLER, Roy P., *et al.*, eds. *A Guide to the Study of the United States of America: Representative Books Reflecting the Development of American Thought and Life.* Washington, D.C., 1960.

3 BEERS, Henry P. *Bibliographies in American History: A Guide to Materials for Research.* Rev. ed., New York, 1942. (A bibliography of bibliographies.)

4 BEMIS, Samuel F. and Grace G. GRIFFIN. *Guide to the Diplomatic History of the United States, 1775-1921.* Washington, D.C., 1935.

5 BOYD, Annie M. *United States Government Publications.* 2d ed. New York, 1941.

6 *Catalogue of Books Represented by Library of Congress Printed Cards.* 167 vols. Ann Arbor, 1942-1946. (This Library of Congress printed catalogue is a basic guide to books and pamphlets. It is to be used in conjunction with the *Supplement* [42 vols. Ann Arbor, 1948], *The Library of Congress Author Catalogue . . . 1948-1952* [24 vols. Ann Arbor, 1953], and *The National Union Catalog* [Ann Arbor, 1961-date], which includes books published after 1952.)

7 *Checklist of United States Public Documents, 1789-1909.* Washington, D.C., 1911.

8 CRICK, Bernard R. and Miriam ALMAN. *A Guide to Manuscripts Relating to America in Great Britain and Ireland.* Oxford, 1961.

9 *Dissertation Abstracts: A Guide to Dissertations and Monographs Available in Microform.* Ann Arbor, 1938-date. (Early volumes were titled *Microfilm Abstracts.*)

10 *Doctoral Dissertations Accepted by American Universities.* 22 vols. New York, 1934-1955.

11 DORNBUSCH, Charles E. *Regimental Publications and Personal Narratives of the Civil War.* 2 vols. to date. New York, 1961-date.

12 *Essay and General Literature Index.* New York, 1934-date.

13 GRIFFIN, Appleton P. C. *Bibliography of American Historical Societies (The United States and the Dominion of Canada). Am Hist Assoc Ann Rep,* 1905, II. Washington, D.C., 1907.

14 HALE, Richard W., Jr., ed. *Guide to Photocopied Historical Materials in the United States and Canada.* Ithaca, 1961.

15 HAMER, Philip M., ed. *A Guide to Archives and Manuscripts in the United States.* New Haven, 1961.

16 HANDLIN, Oscar, *et al.*, eds. *The Harvard Guide to American History.* Cambridge, Mass., 1954.†

17 HOWE, George F., *et al.*, eds. *The American Historical Association's Guide to Historical Literature.* New York, 1961.

18 *International Index to Periodicals.* New York, 1916-date.

19 JOHNSON, Allen and Dumas MALONE, eds. *Dictionary of American Biography.* 22 vols. plus index. New York, 1928-1965.

1 JONES, Joseph, *et al.*, eds. *American Literary Manuscripts: A Checklist of Holdings in Academic, Historical and Public Libraries in the United States.* Austin, Tex., 1960.

2 KEUHL, Warren F. *Dissertations in History: An Index to Dissertations Completed in History Departments of United States and Canadian Universities, 1873-1960.* Lexington, Ky., 1965.

3 LARNED, J. N., ed. *The Literature of American History: A Bibliographical Guide.* Boston, 1902.

4 MUNDEN, Kenneth W. and Henry P. BEERS. *Guide to Federal Archives Relating to the Civil War.* Washington, D.C., 1962.

5 *National Union Catalogue of Manuscript Collections.* 5 vols. to date, plus indexes. Ann Arbor, Hamden, Conn., and Washington, D.C., 1962-date.

6 NEVINS, Allan, James I. ROBERTSON, Jr., and Bell I. WILEY, eds. *Civil War Books: A Critical Bibliography.* 1 vol. to date. Baton Rouge, 1967.

7 *Nineteenth Century Readers' Guide to Periodical Literature, 1890-1899.* 2 vols. New York, 1944.

8 O'NEILL, Edward H. *Biography by Americans, 1658-1936: A Subject Bibliography.* Philadelphia, 1939

9 POOLE, William F., *et al.*, eds. *Poole's Index to Periodical Literature* [1802-1906]. 6 vols. Boston, 1882-1908.

10 POORE, Ben: P. *A Descriptive Catalogue of the Government Publications of the United States, September 5, 1774-March 4, 1881.* Washington, D.C., 1885.

11 *Readers' Guide to Periodical Literature.* New York, 1916-date.

12 SCHMECKEBIER, Laurence F. *Government Publications and Their Use.* Washington, D.C., 1936.

13 SPILLER, Robert E., *et al.*, eds. *Literary History of the United States: Volume III. Bibliography.* New York, 1948. See also the *Bibliographical Supplement,* ed. Richard M. Ludwig (New York, 1959).

14 WINCHELL, Constance M. *Guide to Reference Books.* 8th ed. Chicago, 1967.

15 WOODRESS, James. *Dissertations in American Literature, 1891-1955, with Supplement, 1956-1961.* Durham, N.C., 1962.

16 *Writings on American History.* Princeton, New York, New Haven, and Washington, D.C., 1904-date. Of these annual volumes, that for 1902 was edited by E. C. Richardson and A. E. Morse; that for 1903 by A. C. McLaughlin, *et al.;* those for 1904 and 1905 were never issued; those for 1906-1940 were edited by Grace G. Griffin, *et al.;* those for 1941-1947 were never issued; and those for 1948-1958 were edited by J. R. Masterson. See also the cumulative *Index to the Writings on American History, 1902-1940,* ed. David M. Matteson, *et al.*, Washington, D.C., 1956.

II. General Statistical and Documentary Compilations

17 *American Annual Cyclopaedia and Register of Important Events.* 42 vols. New York, 1862-1903.

18 BAIN, Richard C. *Convention Decisions and Voting Records.* Washington, D.C., 1966.

19 BLACK, Jeremiah S., ed. *Reports of Cases Argued and Determined in the* [United States] *Supreme Court, 1861-62.* 2 vols. Washington, D.C., 1862-1863.

1 BURNHAM, W. D. *Presidential Ballots, 1836-1892.* Baltimore, 1955.

2 *Congressional Globe, Containing the Debates and Proceedings* [of Congress], *1833-1873.* 111 vols. Washington, D.C., 1834-1873.

3 *Historical Statistics of the United States: Colonial Times to 1957.* Washington, D.C., 1960.

4 *Journal of the Executive Proceedings of the Senate of the United States, 1789-1905.* 90 vols. Washington, D.C., 1828-1948.

5 *Journal of the House of Representatives of the United States.* Philadelphia and Washington, D.C., 1789-date.

6 *Journal of the Senate of the United States.* Philadelphia and Washington, D.C., 1789-date.

7 MILLER, Hunter, ed. *Treaties and Other International Acts of the United States of America, 1776-1863.* 8 vols. Washington, D.C., 1931-1948.

8 *Papers Relating to Foreign Relations* [of the United States]. Washington, D.C., 1861-date.

9 PAULLIN, Charles O. *Atlas of the Historical Geography of the United States,* ed. John K. Wright. Washington, D.C., 1932.

10 PORTER, Kirk H. and Donald B. JOHNSON, eds. *National Party Platforms, 1840-1956.* Urbana, 1956.

11 PRESSLY, Thomas J. and William H. SCOFIELD, eds. *Farm Real Estate Values in the United States by Counties, 1850-1959.* Seattle, 1965.

12 RICHARDSON, James D. *A Compilation of the Messages and Papers of the Presidents, 1789-1897.* 10 vols. Washington, D.C., 1896-1899.

13 *Statutes at Large of the United States of America, 1789-1873.* 17 vols. Boston, 1850-1873.

14 *The Tribune Almanac for the Years 1838 to 1868, Inclusive, Comprehending the Politician's Register and the Whig Almanac, Containing Annual Election Returns by States and Counties . . . together with Political Essays, Addresses, Party Platforms, &c. . . .* 2 vols. New York, 1868.

15 WALLACE, J. W. *Cases Argued and Adjudged in the* [United States] *Supreme Court, 1863-1874.* 23 vols. Washington, D.C., 1864-1876.

III. The Causes of the Civil War

16 BEALE, Howard K. "What Historians Have Said About the Causes of the Civil War," in *Theory and Practice in Historical Study.* (Social Science Research Council Bulletin, No. 54.) New York, 1946, 55-102. (Both a masterful survey and an elaborate bibliography.)†

17 BONNER, Thomas N. "Civil War Historians and the Needless War Doctrine." *J Hist Ideas,* XVII (1956), 193-216.

18 CAMPBELL, A. E. "An Excess of Isolation: Isolation and the American Civil War." *J S Hist,* XXIX (1963), 161-174.

19 CAUTHEN, Charles E. and Lewis P. JONES. "The Coming of the Civil War," in *Writing Southern History,* ed. Arthur S. Link and Rembert W. Patrick. Chapel Hill, 1965, pp. 224-248.†

1 CLEBSCH, William A. "Christian Interpretations of the Civil War." *Church Hist* XXX (1961), 212-222.

2 CONWAY, Alan A. *The Causes of the American Civil War: An Historical Perspective.* London, 1961.†

3 CUNLIFFE, Marcus. "The Causes of the American Civil War." *Hist Today,* III (1953), 753-761.

4 DONALD, David. "American Historians and the Causes of the Civil War." *S Atl Q,* LIX (1960), 351-355.

5 DONALD, David. *An Excess of Democracy.* Oxford, 1960.†

6 DRAY, William. "Some Causal Accounts of the American Civil War." *Daedalus,* (Summer, 1962), 578-598.

7 GEYL, Pieter. "The American Civil War and the Problem of Inevitability." *N Eng Q,* XXIV (1951), 147-168.

8 MOFFAT, Charles H. "Conflicting Interpretations as to the Causes of the Civil War." *W Va Hist,* XXIII (1961), 5-14.

9 OWSLEY, Frank L. "The Fundamental Cause of the Civil War: Egocentric Sectionalism." *J S Hist,* VII (1941), 3-18.

10 POTTER, David M. "The Background of the Civil War." *Interpreting and Teaching American History,* ed. William H. Cartwright and Richard L. Watson, Jr. Washington, D.C., 1961, 87-119.

11 PRESSLY, Thomas J. *Americans Interpret Their Civil War.* Princeton, 1954. (A full survey of changing historical interpretations.)†

12 RAMSDELL, Charles W. "The Changing Interpretation of the Civil War." *J S Hist,* III (1937), 3-27.

13 RANDALL, J. G. "The Blundering Generation." *Miss Val Hist Rev,* XXVII (1940), 3-28.

14 ROZWENC, Edwin C., ed. *The Causes of the American Civil War.* Boston, 1961. (A valuable anthology.)†

15 SCHLESINGER, Arthur M., Jr. "The Causes of the Civil War: A Note on Historical Sentimentalism." *Partisan Rev,* XVI (1949), 969-981.

16 STAMPP, Kenneth M., ed. *The Causes of the Civil War.* Englewood Cliffs, 1959. (A useful collection, containing both primary and secondary sources.)†

17 WATERS, William R. "The Economic Basis of the Civil War: A Reappraisal." *Topic,* I (Fall, 1961), 30-39.

IV. The Outbreak of the War: The Sumter Crisis

18 CRAWFORD, Samuel W. *The History of the Fall of Fort Sumter.* New York, 1898.

19 CURRENT, Richard N. "The Confederates and the First Shot." *Hist,* VII (1961), 357-369.

20 CURRENT, Richard N. *Lincoln and the First Shot.* Philadelphia, 1963.†

21 HOOGENBOOM, Ari. "Gustavus Fox and the Relief of Fort Sumter," *C W Hist,* IX (1963), 383-398.

22 JOHNSON, Ludwell H. "Fort Sumter and Confederate Diplomacy." *J S Hist,* XXVI (1960), 441-477.

1 KNOLES, George H., ed. *The Crisis of the Union, 1860-1861.* Baton Rouge, 1965.

2 MEREDITH, Roy. *Storm Over Sumter: The Opening Engagement of the Civil War.* New York, 1957.

3 POTTER, David M. *Lincoln and His Party in the Secession Crisis.* 2d ed., New Haven, 1962.†

4 RAMSDELL, Charles W. "Lincoln and Fort Sumter." *J S Hist,* III (1937), 259-288.

5 RANDALL, J. G. "When War Came in 1861." *A Lincoln Q,* I (1940), 3-42.

6 STAMPP, Kenneth M. *And The War Came: The North and the Secession Crisis, 1860-61.* Baton Rouge, 1950.†

7 STAMPP, Kenneth M. "Lincoln and the Strategy of Defense in the Crisis of 1861." *J S Hist* XI (1945), 297-323.

8 SWANBERG, W. A. *First Blood. The Story of Fort Sumter.* New York, 1958.

9 TILLEY, John S. *Lincoln Takes Command.* Chapel Hill, 1941. (A sharply anti-Lincoln account.)

See also 8.1, 8.2, 8.3, 8.4, 10.6, 10.7, 12.4, 12.5, 12.6, 12.7, 19.3, 21.4, 22.12, 22.14, 29.2, 29.3.

V. Biographies, Autobiographies, Diaries, Letters and Reminiscences of Leaders in the Civil War and Reconstruction Eras

Adams, Charles Francis

10 DUBERMAN, Martin B. *Charles Francis Adams.* Boston, 1961.

11 FORD, Worthington C., ed. *A Cycle of Adams Letters, 1861-1865.* 2 vols. Boston, 1920. (Letters of Charles Francis Adams, Charles Francis Adams, Jr., and Henry Adams.)

Adams, Henry

12 ADAMS, Henry. *The Education of Henry Adams: An Autobiography.* Boston, 1918. (Contains a brilliant discussion of Anglo-American relations during the war.)†

13 FORD, Worthington C., ed. *Letters of Henry Adams, 1858-1891.* Boston, 1930.

14 SAMUELS, Ernest. *Henry Adams: The Middle Years.* Cambridge, Mass., 1958.

15 SAMUELS, Ernest. *The Young Henry Adams.* Cambridge, Mass., 1948.

Alexander, Edward P.

16 ALEXANDER, Edward P. *Military Memoirs of a Confederate,* ed. T. Harry Williams. Bloomington, 1962.

Andrew, John A.

1 PEARSON, Henry G. *The Life of John A. Andrew, Governor of Massachusetts, 1861-1865.* 2 vols. Boston, 1904

Bancroft, George

2 HOWE, M. A. De Wolfe. *The Life and Letters of George Bancroft.* 2 vols. New York, 1908.

3 NYE, Russel B. *George Bancroft: Brahmin Rebel.* New York, 1945.

Banks, Nathaniel P.

4 HARRINGTON, Fred H. *Fighting Politician: Major General N. P. Banks.* Philadelphia, 1948.

Bates, Edward

5 BEALE, Howard K., ed. *The Diary of Edward Bates, 1859-1866.* Washington, D.C., 1933.

6 CAIN, Marvin R. *Lincoln's Attorney General: Edward Bates of Missouri.* Columbia, Mo., 1965.

Beauregard, Pierre G. T.

7 WILLIAMS, T. Harry. *P. G. T. Beauregard: Napoleon in Gray.* Baton Rouge, 1955.†

Bell, John

8 PARKS, Joseph H. *John Bell of Tennessee.* Baton Rouge, 1950.

Belmont, August

9 KATZ, Irving. *August Belmont: A Political Biography.* New York, 1968.

Benjamin, Judah P.

10 MEADE, Robert D. *Judah P. Benjamin: Confederate Statesman.* New York, 1943.

Blaine, James G.

1 BLAINE, James G. *Twenty Years of Congress, from Lincoln to Garfield.* 2 vols. Norwich Conn., 1884-1886.

2 MUZZEY, David S. *James G. Blaine: A Political Idol of Other Days.* New York, 1934.

Blair, Francis P.

3 SMITH, William E. *The Francis Preston Blair Family in Politics.* 2 vols. New York, 1933.

Borcke, Heros von

4 BORCKE, Heros von. *Memoirs of the Confederate War for Independence.* 2 vols. London, 1886.

Bragg, Braxton

5 SEITZ, Don C. *Braxton Bragg, General of the Confederacy.* Columbia, S.C., 1924.

Brown, Joseph E.

6 HILL, Louise B. *Joseph E. Brown and the Confederacy.* Chapel Hill, 1939.

Browning, Orville H.

7 BAXTER, Maurice. *Orville H. Browning: Lincoln's Friend and Critic.* Bloomington, 1957.†

8 PEASE, Theodore C. and James G. RANDALL, eds. *The Diary of Orville Hickman Browning.* 2 vols. Springfield, 1927-33.

Brownlow, William G.

9 COULTER, E. Merton. *William G. Brownlow: Fighting Parson of the Southern Highlands.* Chapel Hill, 1937.

Buchanan, James

1 AUCHAMPAUGH, Philip G. *James Buchanan and His Cabinet on the Eve of Secession.* Lancaster, Pa., 1926.†

2 BUCHANAN, James. *Mr. Buchanan's Administration on the Eve of the Rebellion.* New York, 1866.

3 CURTIS, George T. *Life of James Buchanan.* 2 vols. New York, 1883.

4 KLEIN, Philip S. *President James Buchanan.* University Park, Pa., 1962.

Butler, Benjamin F.

5 BUTLER, Benjamin F. *Autobiography.* Boston, 1892. (Commonly referred to as *Butler's Book.*)

6 JOHNSON, Howard P. "New Orleans under General Butler." *La Hist Q,* XXIV (1941), 434-536.

7 MARSHALL, Jessie A., ed. *Private and Official Correspondence of General Benjamin F. Butler during the Period of the Civil War.* 5 vols. Norwood, Mass., 1917.

8 TREFOUSSE, Hans L. *Ben Butler: The South Called Him Beast!* New York, 1957. (The most scholarly biography.)

9 WEST, Richard S., Jr., *Lincoln's Scapegoat General: A Life of Benjamin F. Butler.* Boston, 1965.

Cameron, Simon

10 BRADLEY, Erwin S. *Simon Cameron: Lincoln's Secretary of War.* Philadelphia, 1966.

Carpenter, Matthew H.

11 THOMPSON, E. Bruce. *Matthew Hale Carpenter, Webster of the West.* Madison, Wis., 1954.

Chandler, William E.

12 RICHARDSON, Leon B. *William E. Chandler, Republican.* New York, 1940.

Chandler, Zachariah

13 HARBISON, Winfred A. "Zachariah Chandler's Part in the Re-election of Abraham Lincoln." *Miss Val Hist Rev,* XXII (1935), 267-276.

14 HARRIS, Wilmer C. *The Public Life of Zachariah Chandler, 1851-1875.* Chicago, 1917.

Chase, Salmon P.

1 DONALD, David, ed. *Inside Lincoln's Cabinet: The Civil War Diaries of Salmon P. Chase.* New York, 1954.

2 HART, Albert B. *Salmon Portland Chase.* Boston, 1899.

3 HUGHES, David F. "Salmon P. Chase: Chief Justice." *Vanderbilt Law Rev,* XVIII (1965), 569-614.

4 SCHUCKERS, J. W. *Life and Public Services of Salmon Portland Chase.* New York, 1874.

5 SMITH, Donnal V. *Chase and Civil War Politics.* Columbus, Ohio, 1931.

6 WARDEN, Robert B. *Private Life and Public Services of Salmon P. Chase.* Cincinnati, 1874.

See also **33**.1, **33**.2, **33**.3.

Chesnut, Mrs. Mary Boykin

7 CHESNUT, Mary Boykin. *A Diary from Dixie,* ed. Ben Ames Williams. Boston, 1949.†

Clay, Cassius M.

8 SMILEY, David L. *Lion of White Hall: The Life of Cassius M. Clay.* Madison, Wis., 1962.

Cobb, Howell

9 MONTGOMERY, Horace. *Howell Cobb's Confederate Career.* Tuscaloosa, 1959.

Colfax, Schuyler

10 HOLLISTER, O. J. *Life of Schuyler Colfax.* New York, 1886.

11 SMITH, Willard H. *Schuyler Colfax: The Changing Fortunes of a Political Idol.* Indianapolis, 1952.

Conkling, Roscoe

12 CHIDSEY, Donald B. *The Gentleman from New York: A Life of Roscoe Conkling.* New Haven, 1935.

13 CONKLING, Alfred R. *The Life and Letters of Roscoe Conkling, Orator, Statesman, Advocate.* New York, 1889.

Cooke, Jay

1 LARSON, Henrietta M. *Jay Cooke, Private Banker.* Cambridge, Mass., 1936.

2 OBERHOLTZER, Ellis P. *Jay Cooke, Financier of the Civil War.* 2 vols. Philadelphia, 1907.

Cox, Jacob D.

3 COX, Jacob D. *Military Reminiscences of the Civil War.* 2 vols. New York, 1900.

Cox, Samuel S.

4 COX, Samuel S. *Three Decades of Federal Legislation, 1855-1885.* 2 vols. Providence, 1885.

5 LINDSEY, David. *"Sunset" Cox: Irrepressible Democrat.* Detroit, 1959.

Crittenden, John J.

6 COLEMAN, Ann M. B. *The Life of John J. Crittenden.* 2 vols. Philadelphia, 1871.

7 KIRWAN, Albert D. *John J. Crittenden: The Struggle for the Union.* Lexington, Ky., 1962.

Cushing, Caleb

8 FUESS, Claude M. *The Life of Caleb Cushing.* 2 vols. New York, 1923.

Custer, George A.

9 MERINGTON, Marguerite, ed. *The Custer Story: The Life and Intimate Letters of General George A. Custer and His Wife Elizabeth.* New York, 1950.

10 MONAGHAN, Jay. Custer: *The Life of General George Armstrong Custer.* Boston, 1959.

Dana, Charles A.

11 DANA, Charles A. *Recollections of the Civil War.* New York, 1902.†

Dana, Richard Henry, Jr.

1 ADAMS, Charles F., Jr. *Richard Henry Dana: A Biography.* 2 vols. Boston, 1890.

2 LUCID, Robert F., ed. *The Journal of Richard Henry Dana, Jr.* 3 vols. Cambridge, Mass., 1968.

3 SHAPIRO, Samuel. *Richard Henry Dana, Jr., 1815-1882.* East Lansing, Mich., 1961.

Davis, David

4 KING, Willard L. *Lincoln's Manager: David Davis.* Cambridge, Mass., 1960.

Davis, Henry Winter

5 STEINER, Bernard C. *Life of Henry Winter Davis.* Baltimore, 1916.

Davis, Jefferson

6 CUTTING, Elizabeth. *Jefferson Davis, Political Soldier.* New York, 1930.

7 DAVIS, Varina H. *Jefferson Davis, Ex-President of the Confederate States of America: A Memoir by His Wife.* 2 vols. New York, 1890.

8 DODD, William E. *Jefferson Davis.* Philadelphia, 1907.

9 ECKENRODE, Hamilton J. *Jefferson Davis, President of the South.* New York, 1923.

10 MC ELROY, Robert. *Jefferson Davis: The Unreal and the Real.* 2 vols. New York 1937.

11 ROWLAND, Dunbar, ed. *Jefferson Davis, Constitutionalist: His Letters, Papers and Speeches.* 10 vols. Jackson, Miss., 1923.

12 STRODE, Hudson. *Jefferson Davis.* 3 vols. New York, 1955-1964. (Though uncritical, the best and fullest biography.)

13 STRODE, Hudson, ed. *Jefferson Davis: Private Letters, 1823-1889.* New York, 1966.

14 WINSTON, Robert W. *High Stakes and Hair Trigger: The Life of Jefferson Davis.* New York, 1930.

DeForest, John W.

15 DEFOREST, John W. *A Union Officer in the Reconstruction,* ed. James H. Croushore and David M. Potter. New Haven, 1948.

16 DEFOREST, John W. *A Volunteer's Adventures: A Union Captain's Record of the Civil War,* ed. James H. Croushore. New Haven, 1946.

DeTrobriand, Regis

17 DETROBRIAND, Regis. *Four Years with the Army of the Potomac.* Boston, 1889.

Dodge, Grenville

1 FARNHAM, Wallace D. "Grenville Dodge and the Union Pacific: A Study of Historical Legends." *J Am Hist*, LI (1965), 632-650.

2 HIRSHSON, Stanley. *Grenville M. Dodge: Soldier, Politician, Railroad Pioneer.* Bloomington, 1967.

Donnelly, Ignatius

3 RIDGE, Martin. *Ignatius Donnelly: The Portrait of a Politician.* Chicago, 1962.

Douglas, Stephen A.

4 CAPERS, Gerald M. *Stephen A. Douglas: Defender of the Union.* Boston, 1959.

5 JOHANNSEN, Robert W., ed. *The Letters of Stephen A Douglas.* Urbana, 1961.

6 JOHNSON, Allen. *Stephen A. Douglas: A Study in American Politics.* New York, 1908.

7 MILTON, George F. *The Eve of Conflict: Stephen A. Douglas and the Needless War.* Boston, 1934.

Douglass, Frederick

8 FONER, Philip S. *The Life and Writings of Frederick Douglass.* 4 vols. New York, 1950-1955.

9 QUARLES, Benjamin. *Frederick Douglass.* Washington, D.C., 1948.

Early, Jubal A.

10 EARLY, Jubal A. *Autobiographical Sketch and Narrative of the War between the States.* Philadelphia, 1912.

Eggleston, George Cary

11 EGGLESTON, George C. *A Rebel's Recollections,* ed. David Donald. Bloomington, 1959.

Ericsson, John

12 CHURCH, William C. *The Life of John Ericsson.* 2 vols. New York, 1890.

13 WHITE, Ruth. *Yankee from Sweden: The Dream and the Reality in the Days of John Ericsson.* New York, 1960.

Evarts, William M.

1 BARROWS, Chester L. *William M. Evarts: Lawyer, Diplomat, Statesman.* Chapel Hill, 1941.

2 DYER, Brainerd. *The Public Career of William M. Evarts.* Berkeley, 1933.

3 EVARTS, William M. *Arguments and Speeches,* ed. Sherman Evarts. 3 vols. New York, 1919.

Everett, Edward

4 FROTHINGHAM, Paul R. *Edward Everett, Orator and Statesman.* Boston, 1925.

Farragut, David G.

5 LEWIS, Charles L. *David Glasgow Farragut.* 2 vols. Annapolis, 1941-1943.

Fessenden, William P.

6 FESSENDEN, Francis. *Life and Public Services of William Pitt Fessenden.* 2 vols. Boston, 1907.

7 JELLISON, Charles A. *Fessenden of Maine: Civil War Senator.* Syracuse, N.Y., 1962.

Field, Stephen J.

8 SWISHER, Carl B. *Stephen J. Field, Craftsman of the Law.* Washington, D.C., 1930.

Fish, Hamilton

9 NEVINS, Allan. *Hamilton Fish: The Inner History of the Grant Administration.* New York, 1936.

Forrest, Nathan B.

10 HENRY, Robert S. *"First With the Most" Forrest.* Indianapolis, 1944.

11 LYTLE, Andrew N. *Bedford Forrest and His Critter Company.* New York, 1931.

Fox, Gustavus V.

1 THOMPSON, R. M. and R. WAINWRIGHT, eds. *Confidential Correspondence of Gustavus Vasa Fox.* 2 vols. New York, 1918.

Fremantle, Arthur J. L.

2 FREMANTLE, Sir Arthur James Lyon. *Three Months in the Southern States: April-June, 1863.* Mobile, 1864.†

Frémont, John C.

3 NEVINS, Allan. *Frémont, Pathmarker of the West.* New York, 1955.

Garfield, James A.

4 BROWN, Harry J. and Frederick D. WILLIAMS, eds. *The Diary of James A. Garfield.* 2 vols. East Lansing, Mich., 1967.

5 CALDWELL, Robert G. *James A. Garfield, Party Chieftain.* New York, 1931.

6 SMITH, Theodore C. *The Life and Letters of James Abram Garfield.* 2 vols. New Haven, 1925.

7 WILLIAMS, Frederick D., ed. *The Wild Life of the Army: Civil War Letters of James A. Garfield.* East Lansing, Mich., 1964.

Garrison, William L.

8 GARRISON, F. J. and W. P. GARRISON. *William Lloyd Garrison, 1805-1879.* 4 vols. New York, 1885.

9 KORNGOLD, Ralph. *Two Friends of Man: The Story of William Lloyd Garrison and Wendell Phillips.* Boston, 1950.

10 MERRILL, Walter M. *Against Wind and Tide.* Cambridge, Mass., 1963.

11 THOMAS, John L. *The Liberator.* Boston, 1963.

Gibbon, John

12 GIBBON, John. *Personal Recollections of the Civil War.* New York, 1928.

Godkin, E. L.

13 OGDEN, Rollo. *Life and Letters of Edwin Lawrence Godkin.* 2 vols. New York, 1907.

15

Gordon, John B.

1 GORDON, John B. *Reminiscences of the Civil War.* New York, 1903.

Gorgas, Josiah

2 VANDIVER, Frank E., ed. *The Civil War Diary of General Josiah Gorgas.* University, Ala., 1947.

3 VANDIVER, Frank E. *Ploughshares into Swords: Josiah Gorgas and Confederate Ordnance.* Austin, Tex., 1952.†

Gould, Jay

4 GRODINSKY, Julius. *Jay Gould: His Business Career, 1867-1892.* Philadelphia, 1957.

Grant, Ulysses S.

5 BADEAU, Adam. *Grant in Peace: From Appomattox to Mount McGregor.* Hartford, 1887.

6 BADEAU, Adam. *Military History of Ulysses S. Grant, from April, 1861, to April, 1865.* 3 vols. New York, 1868-1881.

7 CATTON, Bruce. *Grant Moves South.* Boston, 1960.

8 FULLER, J. F. C. *The Generalship of Ulysses S. Grant.* Bloomington, 1958.

9 GRANT, Ulysses S. *Personal Memoirs of U. S. Grant.* 2 vols. New York, 1885-1886.†

10 HESSELTINE, William B. *Ulysses S. Grant, Politician.* New York, 1935.

11 LEWIS, Lloyd. *Captain Sam Grant.* Boston, 1950.

12 SIMON, John Y., ed. *The Papers of Ulysses S. Grant.* 1 vol. to date. Carbondale, Ill., 1967.

Greeley, Horace

13 FAHRNEY, Ralph R. *Horace Greeley and the Tribune in the Civil War.* Cedar Rapids, Iowa, 1936.

14 GREELEY, Horace. *Recollections of a Busy Life.* New York, 1868.

15 HALE, William H. *Horace Greeley: Voice of the People.* New York, 1950.†

16 VAN DEUSEN, Glyndon G. *Horace Greeley: Nineteenth-Century Crusader.* Philadelphia, 1953.

Grimes, James W.

1 SALTER, William. *The Life of James W. Grimes.* New York, 1876.

Gurowski, Adam

2 FISCHER, LeRoy H. *Lincoln's Gadfly: Adam Gurowski.* Norman, Okla., 1964.

3 GUROWSKI, Adam. *Diary.* 3 vols. Boston, New York, and Washington, D.C., 1862-1866.

Hale, John P.

4 SEWELL, Richard H. *John P. Hale and the Politics of Abolition.* Cambridge, Mass , 1965.

Halleck, Henry W.

5 AMBROSE, Stephen E. *Halleck: Lincoln's Chief of Staff.* Baton Rouge, 1962.

Hamlin, Hannibal

6 HAMLIN, Charles E. *The Life and Times of Hannibal Hamlin.* Cambridge, Mass., 1899.

Hampton, Wade

7 WELLMAN, Manly W. *Giant in Gray: A Biography of Wade Hampton of South Carolina.* New York, 1949.

Hancock, Winfield S.

8 TUCKER, Glenn. *Hancock the Superb.* Indianapolis, 1961.

Hardee, William J.

9 HUGHES, Nathaniel C., Jr. *General William J. Hardee: Old Reliable.* Baton Rouge, 1965.

Harlan, James

10 BRIGHAM, Johnson. *James Harlan.* Iowa City, 1913.

Haupt, Herman

1 HAUPT, Herman. *Reminiscences of General Herman Haupt.* Milwaukee, 1901.

Hay, John

2 DENNETT, Tyler. *John Hay: From Poetry to Politics.* New York, 1933.

3 DENNETT, Tyler, ed. *Lincoln and the Civil War in the Diaries and Letters of John Hay.* New York, 1939.

Hayes, Rutherford B.

4 BARNARD, Harry. *Rutherford B. Hayes and His America.* Indianapolis, 1954.

5 WILLIAMS, C. R. *The Life of Rutherford Birchard Hayes, Nineteenth President of the United States.* 2 vols. Boston, 1914.

6 WILLIAMS, C. R., ed. *Diary and Letters of Rutherford Birchard Hayes.* 5 vols. Columbus, Ohio, 1922-1926.

7 WILLIAMS, T. Harry. *Hayes of the Twenty-Third: The Civil War Volunteer Officer.* New York, 1965.

8 WILLIAMS, T. Harry, ed. *Hayes: The Diary of a President, 1875-1881.* New York, 1964.

Herndon, William H.

9 DONALD, David. *Lincoln's Herndon.* New York, 1948

Hewitt, Abram S.

10 NEVINS, Allan. *Abram S. Hewitt, with Some Account of Peter Cooper.* New York 1935.

11 NEVINS, Allan, ed. *Selected Writings of Abram S. Hewitt.* New York, 1937.

Hicks, Thomas B.

12 RADCLIFFE, George L. P. *Governor Thomas H. Hicks of Maryland and the Civil War.* Baltimore, 1901.

Hill, Benjamin H.

13 PEARCE, Heywood J., Jr. *Benjamin Hill: Secession and Reconstruction.* Chicago, 1928.

Hill, Daniel H.

1 BRIDGES, Hal. *Lee's Maverick General: Daniel Harvey Hill.* New York, 1961.

Hitchcock, Ethan A.

2 CROFFUT, W. A., ed. *Fifty Years in Camp and Field: Diary of Major-General Ethan Allen Hitchcock, U.S.A.* New York, 1909.

Hoar, Ebenezer R.

3 STOREY, Moorfield and Edward W. EMERSON. *Ebenezer Rockwood Hoar: A Memoir.* Boston, 1911.

Hoar, George F.

4 GILLETT, Frederick H. *George Frisbie Hoar.* Boston, 1934.

5 HOAR, George F. *Autobiography of Seventy Years.* 2 vols. New York, 1903.

Holmes, Oliver Wendell

6 HOWE, Mark DeWolfe. *Justice Oliver Wendell Holmes: The Shaping Years, 1841-1870.* Cambridge, Mass., 1957.

7 HOWE, Mark DeWolfe ed. *Touched with Fire: Civil War Letters and Diary of Oliver Wendell Holmes, Jr., 1861-1864.* Cambridge, Mass., 1946.

Hood, John B.

8 DYER, John P. *The Gallant Hood.* Indianapolis, 1950.

9 HOOD, John B. *Advance and Retreat,* ed. Richard N. Current. Bloomington, 1959.

10 O'CONNOR, Richard. *Hood: Cavalier General.* New York, 1949

Hooker, Joseph

11 HEBERT, Walter H. *Fighting Joe Hooker.* Indianapolis, 1944.

Howard, Oliver O.

12 CARPENTER, John A. *Sword and Olive Branch: Oliver Otis Howard.* Pittsburgh, 1964.

1 HOWARD, Oliver O. *Autobiography*. 2 vols. New York, 1903.

2 MC FEELY, William S. *Yankee Stepfather: General O. O. Howard and the Freedmen*. New Haven, 1968.

Jackson, Claiborne F.

3 LYON, William H. "Claiborne Fox Jackson and the Secession Crisis in Missouri." *Mo Hist Rev*, LVIII (1964), 422-441.

Jackson, Thomas J.

4 CHAMBERS, Lenoir. *Stonewall Jackson*. 2 vols. New York, 1959.

5 HENDERSON, G. F. R. *Stonewall Jackson and the American Civil War*. 2 vols. New York, 1919.†

6 VANDIVER, Frank E. *Mighty Stonewall*. New York, 1957.

Johnson, Andrew

7 DEWITT, David M. *Impeachment and Trial of Andrew Johnson*. New York, 1903.

8 GRAF, LeRoy P. and Ralph W. HASKINS, eds. *The Papers of Andrew Johnson*. 1 vol. to date. Knoxville, 1967.

9 HALL, Clifton R. *Andrew Johnson, Military Governor of Tennessee*. Princeton, 1916.

10 MC KITRICK, Eric L. *Andrew Johnson and Reconstruction*. Chicago, 1960.†

11 MILTON, George F. *The Age of Hate: Andrew Johnson and the Radicals*. New York, 1930.

12 STAMPP, Kenneth M. *Andrew Johnson and the Failure of the Agrarian Dream*. Oxford, 1962.†

13 STRYKER, Lloyd P. *Andrew Johnson: A Study in Courage*. New York, 1929.

14 THOMAS, Lately. *The First President Johnson*. New York, 1968.

15 WINSTON, Robert W. *Andrew Johnson, Plebeian and Patriot*. New York, 1928.

See also **61**.5, **61**.7, **61**.9, **61**.10, **61**.11, **61**.12, **61**.13, **61**.14, **61**.15, **62**.1.

Johnson, Reverdy

16 STEINER, Bernard C. *Life of Reverdy Johnson*. Baltimore, 1914.

Johnston, Albert S.

17 ROLAND, Charles P. *Albert Sidney Johnston: Soldier of Three Republics*. Austin, Tex., 1964.

18 JOHNSTON, William P. *The Life of Gen. Albert Sidney Johnston*. New York, 1878.

Johnston, Joseph E.

1 GOVAN, Gilbert E. and James W. LIVINGOOD. *A Different Valor: The Story of General Joseph E. Johnston, C.S.A.* Indianapolis, 1956.

2 JOHNSTON, Joseph E. *Narrative of Military Operations,* ed. Frank E. Vandiver. Bloomington, 1959.

Jones, John B.

3 JONES, J. B. *A Rebel War Clerk's Diary at the Confederate States Capital.* 2 vols. Philadelphia, 1866.†

Julian, George W.

4 CLARKE, Grace J. *George W. Julian.* Indianapolis, 1923.

5 JULIAN, George W. *Political Recollections, 1840 to 1872.* Chicago, 1884.

6 RIDDLEBERGER, Patrick W. *George Washington Julian, Radical Republican.* Indianapolis, 1966.

Kirby Smith, Edmund

7 PARKS, Joseph H. *General Edmund Kirby Smith.* Baton Rouge, 1954

Lamar, L. Q. C.

8 CATE, Wirt A. *Lucius Q. C. Lamar.* Chapel Hill, 1935

Lee, Robert E.

9 BRADFORD, Gamaliel. *Lee the American.* Boston, 1912.

10 DOWDEY, Clifford. *Lee.* Boston, 1965.

11 DOWDEY, Clifford, ed. *The Wartime Papers of R. E. Lee.* Boston, 1961.

12 FREEMAN, Douglas S. *R. E. Lee: A Biography.* 4 vols. New York, 1934-1935. (The fullest and best biography; one of the great works in American historical writing.)

13 MAURICE, Frederick. *Robert E. Lee, the Soldier.* New York, 1925.

14 MIERS, Earl S. *Robert E. Lee: A Great Life in Brief.* New York, 1956. (The best short biography.)†

15 SANBORN, Margaret. *Robert E. Lee.* 2 vols. Philadelphia, 1966-1967. (Volume 1 is an excellent, affectionate portrait; volume 2 is greatly inferior.)

Lieber, Francis

1 FREIDEL, Frank. *Francis Lieber: Nineteenth Century Liberal.* Baton Rouge, 1947.

Lincoln, Abraham

2 ARNOLD, Isaac N. *The Life of Abraham Lincoln.* Chicago, 1885.

3 BALLARD, Colin R. *The Military Genius of Abraham Lincoln.* London, 1926.

4 BARINGER, William E. *A House Dividing: Lincoln as President Elect.* Springfield, Ill., 1945.

5 BARTON, William E. *The Life of Abraham Lincoln.* 2 vols. Indianapolis, 1925.

6 BARTON, William E. *Lincoln at Gettysburg. What He Intended to Say; What He Was Reported to Have Said; What He Wished He Had Said.* Indianapolis, 1930.

7 BASLER, Roy P., ed. *The Collected Works of Abraham Lincoln.* 9 vols. New Brunswick, N.J., 1953-1955. (The definitive edition of Lincoln's writings.)

8 BASLER, Roy P. *The Lincoln Legend: A Study in Changing Conceptions.* Boston, 1935.

9 BISHOP, Jim. *The Day Lincoln Was Shot.* New York, 1955. (A vivid, journalistic account.)†

10 BROOKS, Noah. *Washington in Lincoln's Time.* New York, 1895. (Colorful reminiscences by one of Lincoln's private secretaries.)

11 BROWNE, Francis F., ed. *The Every-Day Life of Abraham Lincoln.* 2d ed. Chicago, 1913.

12 BRUCE, Robert V. *Lincoln and the Tools of War.* Indianapolis, 1956.

13 CARMAN, Harry J. and Reinhard H. LUTHIN. *Lincoln and the Patronage.* New York, 1943.

14 CARPENTER, Francis B. *Six Months at the White House with Abraham Lincoln: The Story of a Picture.* New York, 1866. (Affectionate memoir by the artist who painted the President reading the Emancipation Proclamation.)

15 CHARNWOOD, Lord. *Abraham Lincoln.* London, 1917.†

16 CURRENT, Richard N. *The Lincoln Nobody Knows: A Portrait in Contrast of the Greatest American.* New York, 1958. (Stimulating essays on the paradoxes in Lincoln's career.)†

17 DEWITT, David M. *The Assassination of Abraham Lincoln and Its Expiation.* New York, 1909. (Still the most reliable account.)

18 DONALD, David. *Lincoln Reconsidered: Essays on the Civil War Era.* New York, 1956.†

19 DONALD, David. *Lincoln's Herndon.* New York, 1948. (Both a biography of Lincoln's law partner and a study of the changing historical reputation of Lincoln.)

20 EISENSCHIML, Otto. *Why Was Lincoln Murdered?* Boston, 1937. (A full account of the assassination plot, but one that casts unwarranted suspicion on Stanton.)†

1 HAMILTON, Charles and Lloyd OSTENDORF. *Lincoln in Photographs: An Album of Every Known Pose.* Norman, Okla., 1963.

2 HARPER, Robert S. *Lincoln and the Press.* New York, 1951.

3 HENDRICK, Burton J. *Lincoln's War Cabinet.* Boston, 1946.†

4 HERNDON, William H. and Jesse W. WEIK. *Herndon's Lincoln: The True Story of a Great Life.* 3 vols. Chicago, 1889. (Critical biography by Lincoln's law partner.)†

5 HESSELTINE, William B. *Lincoln and the War Governors.* New York, 1948.

6 HOLLAND, Josiah G. *The Life of Abraham Lincoln.* Springfield, Mass., 1866.

7 HOWELLS, William D. *Lives and Speeches of Abraham Lincoln and Hannibal Hamlin.* Columbus, Ohio, 1860. (Campaign biography by the future novelist.)

8 JOHNSON, Ludwell H. "Lincoln and Equal Rights: The Authenticity of the Wadsworth Letter." *J S Hist,* XXXII (1966), 83-87. (Exposes alleged Lincoln letter calling for Negro suffrage.)

9 KEMPF, Edward J. *Abraham Lincoln's Philosophy of Common Sense: An Analytical Biography of a Great Mind.* 3 vols. New York, 1965. (A ponderous attempt to psychoanalyze Lincoln.)

10 LAMON, Ward H. *The Life of Abraham Lincoln from His Birth to His Inauguration as President.* Boston, 1872. (Sharply critical biography, based on materials supplied by Herndon and written by C. F. Black.)

11 LEWIS, Lloyd. *Myths after Lincoln.* New York, 1929.†

12 LUTHIN, Reinhard H. *The First Lincoln Campaign.* Cambridge, Mass., 1944.

13 LUTHIN, Reinhard H. *The Real Abraham Lincoln.* Englewood Cliffs, 1960.

14 MEARNS, David C., ed. *The Lincoln Papers.* 2 vols. Garden City, N.Y., 1948. (Selections from the Robert Todd Lincoln manuscripts.)

15 MILTON, George F. *Abraham Lincoln and the Fifth Column.* New York, 1942.†

16 MITGANG, Herbert, ed. *Lincoln As They Saw Him.* New York, 1956. (Useful samplings of newspaper opinion.)†

17 MONAGHAN, Jay. *Diplomat in Carpet Slippers: Abraham Lincoln Deals with Foreign Affairs.* Indianapolis, 1945.†

18 MONAGHAN, Jay, ed. *Lincoln Bibliography, 1839-1939.* 2 vols. Springfield, Ill., 1945. (The definitive listing.)

19 NICOLAY, John G. and John HAY. *Abraham Lincoln: A History.* 10 vols. New York, 1890. (Massive, full-scale biography by two of the President's secretaries.)†

20 PARGELLIS, Stanley. "Lincoln's Political Philosophy." *A Lincoln Q,* III (1945), 275-290.

21 PRATT, Harry E., ed. *Concerning Mr. Lincoln: In Which Abraham Lincoln Is Pictured as He Appeared to Letter Writers of His Time.* Springfield, Ill., 1944.

22 PRATT, Harry E. *The Personal Finances of Abraham Lincoln.* Springfield, Ill., 1943.

23 PRESSLY, Thomas J. "Bullets and Ballots: Lincoln and the 'Right of Revolution'." *Am Hist Rev,* LVII (1962), 647-662.

24 QUARLES, Benjamin. *Lincoln and the Negro.* New York, 1962.

25 RANDALL, J. G. *Constitutional Problems under Lincoln.* Rev. ed. Urbana, 1951. (The definitive study, of far broader implications than its title might indicate.)†

1 RANDALL, J. G. *Lincoln and the South.* Baton Rouge, 1946.

2 RANDALL, J. G. *Lincoln the Liberal Statesman.* New York, 1947. (Broad-ranging essays on various aspects of Lincoln's career.)†

3 RANDALL, J. G. and Richard N. CURRENT. *Lincoln the President.* 4 vols. New York, 1945-1955. (The most scholarly and analytical study of Lincoln's presidential years.)†

4 RANDALL, Ruth P. *Lincoln's Sons.* Boston, 1956.

5 RAWLEY, James A. "The Nationalism of Abraham Lincoln." *C W Hist,* IX (1963), 283-298.

6 RICE, Allen T., ed. *Reminiscences of Abraham Lincoln by Distinguished Men of His Time.* New York, 1886.

7 ROSCOE, Theodore. *The Web of Conspiracy.* Englewood Cliffs, 1960. (A detailed account of the assassination conspiracy, which unwarrantably implicates Stanton.)

8 SANDBURG, Carl. *Abraham Lincoln: The War Years.* 4 vols. New York, 1939. (The longest, fullest, and most humanly interpretive of the Lincoln biographies.)†

9 SEGAL, Charles M., ed. *Conversations with Lincoln.* New York, 1961.

10 SHAW, Archer H., ed. *The Lincoln Encyclopedia: The Spoken and Written Words of A. Lincoln, Arranged for Ready Reference.* New York, 1950. (A valuable tool which, however, contains some spurious entries.)

11 SILVER, David M. *Lincoln's Supreme Court.* Urbana, 1956.†

12 TARBELL, Ida M. *The Life of Abraham Lincoln.* 2 vols. New York, 1900.

13 THOMAS, Benjamin P. *Abraham Lincoln.* New York, 1952. (The outstanding one-volume biography.)

14 THOMAS, Benjamin P. *Portrait for Posterity: Lincoln and His Biographers.* New Brunswick, N.J., 1947.

15 WEIK, Jesse W. *The Real Lincoln: A Portrait.* Cambridge, Mass., 1922.

16 WILLIAMS, T. Harry. *Lincoln and His Generals.* New York, 1952. (A spirited, scholarly account of Lincoln's difficulties with, and growing ascendency over, the military.)†

17 WILLIAMS, T. Harry. *Lincoln and the Radicals.* Madison, Wis., 1941. (A basic study of Civil War politics.)†

18 WILSON, Rufus R. *Lincoln in Caricature.* Elmira, 1945.

19 WOLDMAN, Albert A. *Lincoln and the Russians.* Cleveland, 1952.†

20 WOLF, William J. *The Religion of Abraham Lincoln.* New York, 1963.

21 ZORNOW, William F. *Lincoln and the Party Divided.* Norman, Okla., 1954. (A scholarly study of the 1864 election.)

See also **4**.19, **5**.3, **5**.4, **5**.7, **5**.9, **17**.2, **17**.3, **17**.9.

Lincoln, Mary

22 EVANS, William A. *Mrs. Abraham Lincoln: A Study of Her Personality and Her Influence on Lincoln.* New York, 1932.

23 RANDALL, Ruth P. *Mary Lincoln: Biography of a Marriage.* Boston, 1953. (A sympathetic, superbly written study that casts much light on Lincoln.)†

24 SANDBURG, Carl and Paul M. ANGLE. *Mary Lincoln: Wife and Widow.* New York, 1949. (Contains many documents and letters.)

Littlefield, Milton S.

1 DANIELS, Jonathan. *Prince of Carpetbaggers.* Philadelphia, 1958.

Logan, John A.

2 DAWSON, George F. *Life and Services of Gen. John A. Logan.* Chicago, 1887.

3 JONES, James P. *"Black Jack": John A. Logan and Southern Illinois in the Civil War Era.* Tallahassee, 1967.

4 LOGAN, John A. *The Volunteer Soldier of America . . . with Memoir of the Author . . . .* Chicago, 1877.

Longstreet, James

5 ECKENRODE, H. J. and Bryan CONRAD. *James Longstreet: Lee's War Horse.* Chapel Hill, 1935.

6 LONGSTREET, James. *From Manassas to Appomattox: Memoirs of the Civil War in America.* Philadelphia, 1896.

7 SANGER, Donald B. and Thomas R. HAY. *James Longstreet.* Baton Rouge, 1952.

Lovejoy, Owen

8 MAGDOL, Edward. *Owen Lovejoy: Abolitionist in Congress.* New Brunswick, N.J., 1967.

Lowell, James Russell

9 DUBERMAN, Martin. *James Russell Lowell.* Boston, 1966.

10 NORTON, Charles E., ed. *Letters of James Russell Lowell.* 2 vols. New York, 1894.

McClellan, George B.

11 ECKENRODE, H. J. and Bryan CONRAD. *George B. McClellan: The Man Who Saved the Union.* Chapel Hill, 1941.

12 HASSLER, Warren W., Jr. *General George B. McClellan: Shield of the Union.* Baton Rouge, 1957. (The best modern defense of McClellan.)

13 MC CLELLAN, George B. *McClellan's Own Story.* New York, 1886.

14 MYERS, William S. *A Study in Personality: General George Brinton McClellan.* New York, 1934.

McCormick, Cyrus H.

1 HUTCHINSON, William T. *Cyrus Hall McCormick.* 2 vols. New York, 1930-1935.

McCulloch, Hugh

2 MC CULLOCH, Hugh. *Men and Measures of Half a Century.* New York, 1888.

Mahone, William

3 BLAKE, Nelson M. *William Mahone of Virginia: Soldier and Political Insurgent.* Richmond, 1935.

Mallory, Stephen R.

4 DURKIN, Joseph T. *Stephen R. Mallory: Confederate Navy Chief.* Chapel Hill, 1954.

Marsh, George P.

5 LOWENTHAL, David. *George Perkins Marsh: Versatile Vermonter.* New York, 1958.

Mason, James M.

6 MASON, Virginia. *The Public Life . . . of James M. Mason.* Roanoke, 1903.

Maury, Matthew F.

7 WILLIAMS, Francis L. *Matthew Fontaine Maury: Scientist of the Sea.* New Brunswick, N.J., 1963.

Meade, George G.

8 AGASSIZ, George R., ed. *Meade's Headquarters, 1863-1865: Letters of Colonel Theodore Lyman from the Wilderness to Appomattox.* Boston, 1922.

9 CLEAVES, Freeman. *Meade of Gettysburg.* Norman, Okla., 1960.

10 MEADE, George, Jr. *The Life and Letters of George Gordon Meade, Major General, United States Army.* 2 vols. New York, 1913.

Meigs, Montgomery C.

1 WEIGLEY, Russell F. *Quartermaster General of the Union Army: A Biography of M. C. Meigs.* New York, 1959.

Memminger, Christopher G.

2 CAPERS, H. D. *The Life and Times of C. G. Memminger.* Richmond, 1893.

Miller, Samuel F.

3 FAIRMAN, Charles. *Mr. Justice Miller and the Supreme Court, 1864-1890.* Cambridge, Mass., 1939.

Moran, Benjamin

4 WALLACE, Sarah A. and Frances E. GILLESPIE, eds. *The Journal of Benjamin Moran, 1857-1865.* 2 vols. Chicago, 1948-1949.

Morgan, Edwin D.

5 RAWLEY, James A. *Edwin D. Morgan, 1811-1883.* New York, 1955.

Morgan, John H.

6 HOLLAND, Cecil F. *Morgan and His Raiders.* New York, 1942.

7 SWIGGETT, Howard. *The Rebel Raider: A Life of John Hunt Morgan.* Garden City, N.Y., 1937.

Morrill, Justin S.

8 PARKER, William B. *The Life and Public Services of Justin Smith Morrill.* Boston, 1924.

Morton, Oliver P.

9 FOULKE, William D. *Life of Oliver P. Morton, Including His Important Speeches.* 2 vols. Indianapolis, 1899.

Mosby, John S.

1 JONES, Virgil C. *Ranger Mosby.* Chapel Hill, 1944.

2 MOSBY, John S. *The Memoirs of Colonel John S. Mosby,* ed. Charles W. Russell. Boston, 1917.

Motley, John L.

3 CURTIS, George W., ed. *The Correspondence of John Lothrop Motley.* 2 vols. New York, 1889.

4 LYNCH, Claire. *The Diplomatic Mission of John Lothrop Motley to Austria, 1861-1867.* Washington, D.C., 1944.

Nast, Thomas

5 KELLER, Morton. *The Art and Politics of Thomas Nast.* New York, 1968.

6 PAINE, Albert B. *Thomas Nast: His Period and His Pictures.* New York, 1904.

Owen, Robert Dale

7 LEOPOLD, Richard W. *Robert Dale Owen: A Biography.* Cambridge, Mass., 1940.

Patrick, Marsena R.

8 SPARKS, David S., ed. *Inside Lincoln's Army: The Diary of Marsena Rudolph Patrick, Provost Marshal General, Army of the Potomac.* New York, 1964.

Pemberton, John C.

9 PEMBERTON, John C. *Pemberton: Defender of Vicksburg.* Chapel Hill, 1942.

Perry, Benjamin F.

10 KIBLER, Lillian A. *Benjamin F. Perry: South Carolina Unionist.* Durham, N.C., 1946.

Phillips, Wendell

11 BARTLETT, Irving H. *Wendell Phillips: Brahmin Radical.* Boston, 1962.

12 SHERWIN, Oscar. *Prophet of Liberty: The Life and Times of Wendell Phillips.* New York, 1958.

Pierpont, Francis H.

1 AMBLER, Charles H. *Francis H. Pierpont: Union War Governor of Virginia and Father of West Virginia.* Chapel Hill, 1937.

Pike, James S.

2 DURDEN, Robert F. *James Shepherd Pike: Republicanism and the American Negro, 1850-1882.* Durham, N.C., 1957.

Pinchback, P. B. S.

3 GROSZ, Agnes S. "The Political Career of Pinckney Benton Stewart Pinchback." *La Hist Q,* XXVII (1944), 527-612.

Polk, Leonidas

4 PARKS, Joseph H. *General Leonidas Polk, C.S.A.: The Fighting Bishop.* Baton Rouge, 1962.

5 POLK, William M. *Leonidas Polk: Bishop and General.* 2 vols. New York, 1915.

Porter, David D.

6 PORTER, David D. *Incidents and Anecdotes of the Civil War.* New York, 1886.

7 SOLEY, James R. *Admiral Porter.* New York, 1903.

8 WEST, Richard S., Jr. *The Second Admiral: A Life of David Dixon Porter.* New York, 1937.

Porter, Fitz John

9 EISENSCHIML, Otto. *The Celebrated Case of Fitz John Porter: An American Dreyfus Affair.* Indianapolis, 1950.

Porter, Horace

10 PORTER, Horace. *Campaigning with Grant.* New York, 1897.

Price, Sterling

1 CASTEL, Albert. *General Sterling Price and the Civil War in the West.* Baton Rouge, 1968.

"Public Man" (pseud.)

2 ANDERSON, Frank M. *The Mystery of "A Public Man": A Historical Detective Story.* Minneapolis, 1948. (Casts serious doubt upon the authenticity of the so-called "Diary.")

3 BULLARD, F. Lauriston, ed. *The Diary of a Public Man. . . .* New Brunswick, N.J., 1946. (A presumed diary, kept during the secession crisis, first published in 1879.)

Quantril, William C.

4 CASTEL, Albert. *William Clarke Quantril: His Life and Times.* New York, 1962.

Rawlins, John A.

5 WILSON, James H. *The Life of John A. Rawlins: Lawyer, Assistant Adjutant-General, Chief of Staff, Major General of Volunteers, and Secretary of War.* New York, 1916.

Raymond, Henry J.

6 BROWN, Francis. *Raymond of the Times.* New York, 1951.

7 DODD, Dorothy. *Henry J. Raymond and the New York Times during Reconstruction.* Chicago, 1936.

Reagan, John H.

8 PROCTER, Ben H. *Not Without Honor: The Life of John H. Reagan.* Austin, Tex., 1962.

9 REAGAN, John H. *Memoirs, with Special Reference to Secession and the Civil War,* ed. Walter F. McCaleb. New York, 1906.

Reid, Whitelaw

10 CORTISSOZ, Royal. *The Life of Whitelaw Reid.* 2 vols. New York, 1921.

Rockefeller, John D.

11 NEVINS, Allan. *Study in Power: John D. Rockefeller, Industrialist and Philanthropist.* 2 vols. New York, 1953.

Rosecrans, William S.

1 LAMERS, William M. *The Edge of Glory: A Biography of General William S. Rosecrans, U.S.A.* New York, 1961.

Ruffin, Edmund

2 CRAVEN, Avery O. *Edmund Ruffin, Southerner: A Study in Secession.* New York, 1932.†

Russell, William Howard

3 RUSSELL, William Howard. *My Diary, North and South.* Boston, 1863.†

Schofield, John M.

4 SCHOFIELD, John M. *Forty-Six Years in the Army.* New York, 1897.

Schurz, Carl

5 BANCROFT, Frederic, ed. *Speeches, Correspondence and Political Papers of Carl Schurz.* 6 vols. New York, 1913.

6 FUESS, Claude M. *Carl Schurz, Reformer (1829-1906).* New York, 1932.

7 SCHAFER, Joseph, ed. *Intimate Letters of Carl Schurz, 1841-1869.* Madison, Wis., 1928.

8 SCHURZ, Carl. *The Reminiscences of Carl Schurz.* 3 vols. New York, 1907-1908.

Scott, Thomas

9 KAMM, Samuel R. *The Civil War Career of Thomas A. Scott.* Philadelphia, 1940.

Scott, Winfield

10 ELLIOTT, Charles W. *Winfield Scott: The Soldier and the Man.* New York, 1937.

Seddon, James A.

11 CURRY, Roy W. "James A. Seddon, A Southern Prototype." *Va Mag Hist & Biog,* LXIII (1955), 123-150.

Semmes, Raphael

1 MERIWETHER, Colyer. *Raphael Semmes.* Philadelphia, 1913.

2 ROBERTS, W. Adolphe. *Semmes of the Alabama.* Indianapolis, 1938.

3 SEMMES, Raphael. *Service Afloat; or, The Remarkable Career of the Confederate Cruisers, Sumter and Alabama, during the War between the States.* Baltimore, 1887.†

Seward, Frederick W.

4 SEWARD, Frederick W. *Reminiscences of a War-Time Statesman and Diplomat, 1830-1915.* New York, 1916.

Seward, William H.

5 BAKER, George E., ed. *The Works of William H. Seward.* 5 vols. New York and Boston, 1853-1884.

6 BANCROFT, Frederic. *The Life of William H. Seward.* 2 vols. New York, 1900.

7 SEWARD, Frederick W., ed. *William H. Seward: An Autobiography from 1801 to 1834, with a Memoir of His Life, and Selections from His Letters.* 3 vols. New York, 1891.

8 VAN DEUSEN, Glyndon G. *William Henry Seward.* New York, 1967.

Seymour, Horatio

9 MITCHELL, Stewart. *Horatio Seymour of New York.* Cambridge, Mass., 1938.

Sheridan, Philip H.

10 O'CONNOR, Richard. *Sheridan the Inevitable.* Indianapolis, 1953.

11 SHERIDAN, Philip H. *Personal Memoirs of P. H. Sheridan.* 2 vols. New York, 1888.

Sherman, John

12 BURTON, Theodore E. *John Sherman.* Boston, 1906.

13 RANDALL, J. G. "John Sherman and Reconstruction." *Miss Val Hist Rev,* XIX (1932), 382-393.

14 SHERMAN, John. *John Sherman's Recollections of Forty Years in the House, Senate and Cabinet: An Autobiography.* 2 vols. Chicago, 1895.

Sherman, William T.

1 HOWE, M. A. DeWolfe, ed. *Home Letters of General Sherman.* New York, 1909.

2 LEWIS, Lloyd. *Sherman, Fighting Prophet.* New York, 1932.

3 LIDDELL HART, Basil H. *Sherman: Soldier, Realist, American.* New York, 1929.†

4 MIERS, Earl S. *The General Who Marched to Hell: William Tecumseh Sherman and His March to Fame and Infamy.* New York, 1951.†

5 SHERMAN, William T. *Memoirs of General W. T. Sherman, Written by Himself.* 2 vols. 2d ed. New York, 1887.†

6 THORNDIKE, Rachel S., ed. *The Sherman Letters: Correspondence between General and Senator Sherman from 1837 to 1891.* New York, 1894.

Sickles, Daniel

7 SWANBERG, W. A. *Sickles the Incredible.* New York, 1956.

Simpson, Matthew

8 CLARK, Robert D. *The Life of Matthew Simpson.* New York, 1956.

Slidell, John

9 SEARS, Louis M. *John Slidell.* Durham, N.C., 1925.

10 WILLSON, Beckles. *John Slidell and the Confederates in Paris (1862-65).* New York, 1932.

Smith, William F.

11 SMITH, William F. *From Chattanooga to Petersburg under Generals Grant and Butler.* Boston, 1893.

Sorrel, G. Moxley

12 SORREL, G. Moxley. *Recollections of a Confederate Staff Officer.* New York, 1905.

Sprague, Kate Chase

1 BELDEN, Thomas G. and Marva R. BELDEN. *So Fell the Angels.* Boston, 1956. (A joint biography of Kate Chase, her father, Chief Justice Chase, and her husband, Senator Sprague.)

2 PHELPS, Mary M. *Kate Chase, Dominant Daughter: The Story of a Brilliant Woman and Her Famous Father.* New York, 1935.

3 ROSS, Ishbel. *Proud Kate: Portrait of an Ambitious Woman.* New York, 1953.

Stanton, Edwin M.

4 FLOWER, Frank A. *Edwin McMasters Stanton: Lincoln's Great War Secretary.* New York, 1905.

5 GORHAM, George C. *Life and Public Services of Edwin M. Stanton.* 2 vols. Boston, 1899.

6 PRATT, Fletcher. *Stanton: Lincoln's Secretary of War.* New York, 1953.

7 THOMAS, Benjamin P. and Harold M. HYMAN. *Stanton: The Life and Times of Lincoln's Secretary of War.* New York, 1962.

Stephens, Alexander H.

8 CLEVELAND, Henry. *Alexander H. Stephens, in Public and Private.* Philadelphia, 1866.

9 JOHNSTON, Richard M. and William H. BROWNE. *Life of Alexander H. Stephens.* Philadelphia, 1878.

10 RABUN, James Z. "Alexander H. Stephens and Jefferson Davis." *Am Hist Rev,* LVIII (1953), 290-321.

11 RICHARDSON, E. Ramsay. *Little Aleck: A Life of Alexander H. Stephens, the Fighting Vice-President of the Confederacy.* Indianapolis, 1932.

12 STEPHENS, Alexander H. *A Constitutional View of the Late War Between the States.* 2 vols. Chicago, 1868-1870.

13 STEPHENS, Alexander H. *Recollections of Alexander H. Stephens.* New York, 1910.

14 VON ABELE, Rudolph. *Alexander H. Stephens: A Biography.* New York, 1946.

Stevens, Thaddeus

15 BRODIE, Fawn M. *Thaddeus Stevens: Scourge of the South.* New York, 1959.†

16 CURRENT, Richard N. *Old Thad Stevens: A Story of Ambition.* Madison, Wis. 1942

17 KORNGOLD, Ralph. *Thaddeus Stevens: A Being Darkly Wise and Rudely Great.* New York, 1955.

1 SINGMASTER, Elsie. *I Speak for Thaddeus Stevens.* Boston, 1947.

2 WOODBURN, James A. *The Life of Thaddeus Stevens: A Study in American Political History.* Indianapolis, 1913.

Strong, George Templeton

3 NEVINS, Allan and Milton H. THOMAS, eds. *The Diary of George Templeton Strong, 1835-1875.* 4 vols. New York, 1952.

Stuart, J. E. B.

4 DAVIS, Burke. *Jeb Stuart: The Last Cavalier.* New York, 1957.

5 THOMASON, John W., Jr. *Jeb Stuart.* New York, 1930.

Sumner, Charles

6 DONALD, David. *Charles Sumner and the Coming of the Civil War.* New York, 1960.

7 PIERCE, Edward L. *Memoir and Letters of Charles Sumner.* 4 vols. Boston, 1877-1893.

8 SUMNER, Charles. *Works.* 15 vols. Boston, 1870-1883.

Taney, Roger B.

9 LEWIS, Walker. *Without Fear or Favor: A Biography of Chief Justice Roger Brooke Taney.* Boston, 1965.

10 SWISHER, Carl B. *Roger B. Taney.* New York, 1935.

Taylor, Richard

11 TAYLOR, Richard. *Destruction and Reconstruction: Personal Experiences of the Late War.* New York, 1879.

Thomas, George H.

12 CLEAVES, Freeman. *Rock of Chattanooga: The Life of General George H. Thomas.* Norman, Okla., 1948.

13 MC KINNEY, Francis F. *Education in Violence: The Life of George H. Thomas and the History of the Army of the Cumberland.* Detroit, 1961.

Tilden, Samuel J.

1 BIGELOW, John. *The Life of Samuel J. Tilden.* 2 vols. New York, 1895.

2 FLICK, Alexander C. *Samuel Jones Tilden: A Study in Political Sagacity.* New York, 1939.

3 HIRSCH, Mark D. "Samuel J. Tilden: The Story of a Lost Opportunity." *Am Hist Rev,* LVI (1951), 788-802.

Toombs, Robert

4 PHILLIPS, Ulrich B. *The Life of Robert Toombs.* New York, 1913.

5 PHILLIPS, Ulrich B., ed. *The Correspondence of Robert Toombs, Alexander H. Stephens, and Howell Cobb. Ann Rep Am Hist Assoc,* 1911, vol. 2. Washington, D.C., 1913.

6 THOMPSON, William Y. *Robert Toombs of Georgia.* Baton Rouge, 1966.

Tourgée, Albion W.

7 GROSS, Theodore L. *Albion W. Tourgée.* New York, 1963.

8 OLSEN, Otto H. *Carpetbagger's Crusade: The Life of Albion Winegar Tourgee.* Baltimore, 1965.

Trumbull, Lyman

9 KRUG, Mark M. *Lyman Trumbull, Conservative Radical.* New York, 1965.

10 WHITE, Horace. *The Life of Lyman Trumbull.* Boston, 1913.

Tweed, William M.

11 LYNCH, Denis T. *"Boss" Tweed.* New York, 1927.

Upton, Emory

12 AMBROSE, Stephen E. *Upton and the Army.* Baton Rouge, 1964.

Usher, John P.

13 RICHARDSON, Elmo R. and Alan W. FARLEY. *John Palmer Usher: Lincoln's Secretary of the Interior.* Lawrence, Kan., 1960.

Vallandigham, Clement L.

1 VALLANDIGHAM, James L. *A Life of Clement L. Vallandigham.* Baltimore, 1872.

Vance, Zebulon B.

2 JOHNSTON, Frontis W., ed. *The Papers of Zebulon Baird Vance.* 1 vol. to date. Raleigh, 1963.

3 TUCKER, Glenn. *Zeb Vance: Champion of Personal Freedom.* Indianapolis, 1966.

4 YATES, Richard E. *The Confederacy and Zeb Vance.* Tuscaloosa, 1958.

Van Dorn, Earl

5 HARTJE, Robert G. *Van Dorn: The Life and Times of a Confederate General.* Nashville, 1967.

Wade, Benjamin F.

6 RIDDLE, Albert G. *Life of Benjamin F. Wade.* Cleveland, 1886.

7 TREFOUSSE, Hans L. *Benjamin Franklin Wade: Radical Republican from Ohio.* New York, 1963.

Wadsworth, James S.

8 PEARSON, Henry G. *James S. Wadsworth of Geneseo, Brevet Major-General of United States Volunteers.* New York, 1913.

Walker, Leroy P.

9 HARRIS, William C. *Leroy Pope Walker: Confederate Secretary of War.* Tuscaloosa, 1962.

Warmoth, Henry C.

10 WARMOTH, Henry C. *War, Politics, and Reconstruction: Stormy Days in Louisiana.* New York, 1930

Warren, Gouverneur K.

11 TAYLOR, Emerson G. *Gouverneur Kemble Warren: The Life and Letters of an American Soldier, 1830-1882.* Boston, 1932.

Watterson, Henry

1 WALL, Joseph F. *Henry Watterson: Reconstructed Rebel.* New York, 1956.

2 WATTERSON, Henry. *"Marse Henry": An Autobiography.* 2 vols. New York, 1919.

Wayne, James M.

3 LAWRENCE, Alexander A. *James Moore Wayne: Southern Unionist.* Chapel Hill, 1943.

Weed, Thurlow

4 VAN DEUSEN, Glyndon G. *Thurlow Weed: Wizard of the Lobby.* Boston, 1947.

5 WEED, Harriet A. and Thurlow Weed BARNES, eds. *Life of Thurlow Weed, including His Autobiography and a Memoir.* 2 vols. Boston, 1883-1884.

Welles, Gideon

6 MORDELL, Albert, ed. *Selected Essays by Gideon Welles: Civil War and Reconstruction.* New York, 1959.

7 WELLES, Gideon. *Diary of Gideon Welles, Secretary of the Navy under Lincoln and Johnson,* ed. Howard K. Beale and Alan W. Brownsword. 3 vols. New York, 1960.

8 WEST, Richard S., Jr. *Gideon Welles: Lincoln's Navy Department.* New York, 1943.

Wheeler, Joseph

9 DYER, John P. *"Fightin' Joe" Wheeler.* Baton Rouge, 1941.

Wilson, James H.

10 WILSON, James H. *Under the Old Flag: Recollections of Military Operations in the War for the Union, the Spanish War, the Boxer Rebellion.* New York, 1912.

Winslow, John A.

11 ELLICOTT, John M. *The Life of John Ancrum Winslow, Rear Admiral United States Navy.* New York, 1902.

Wood, Fernando

12 PLEASANTS, Samuel A. *Fernando Wood of New York.* New York, 1948.

Worth, Jonathan

1 ZUBER, Richard L. *Jonathan Worth: A Biography of a Southern Unionist.* Chapel Hill, 1965.

Yancey, William L.

2 DUBOSE, John W. *The Life and Times of William Lowndes Yancey.* 2 vols. Birmingham, 1892.

Yates, Richard

3 YATES, Richard and Catherine Yates PICKERING. *Richard Yates: Civil War Governor,* ed. John H. Krenkel. Danville, Ill., 1966.

VI. General Works on the Civil War

4 ABEL, Annie H. *The American Indian as Participant in the Civil War.* Cleveland, 1919.

5 BARKER, Alan. *The Civil War in America.* Garden City, NY., 1961.†

6 BASLER, Roy P. *A Short History of the American Civil War.* New York, 1967.

7 BOATNER, Mark M., III. *The Civil War Dictionary.* New York, 1959.

8 CATTON, Bruce. *The Centennial History of the Civil War.* 3 vols. Garden City, N.Y., 1961-1965. (A sweeping narrative treatment, full of personality sketches and battle scenes.)†

9 CATTON, Bruce. *This Hallowed Ground: The Story of the Union Side of the Civil War.* Garden City, N.Y., 1956. (One of the best one-volume treatments, strongest on military affairs.)†

10 CHANNING, Edward. *The War for Southern Independence (A History of the United States,* VI). New York, 1925. (Authoritative and valuable topical treatment, with excellent bibliographical annotations.)

11 COLE, Arthur C. *The Irrepressible Conflict, 1850-1865.* New York, 1934. (A broad survey of social and economic developments.)

12 COMMAGER, Henry S., ed. *The Blue and the Gray: The Story of the Civil War as Told by Participants.* 2 vols. Indianapolis, 1950.

13 DONALD, David, ed. *Divided We Fought: A Pictorial History of the War, 1861-1865.* New York, 1952.

14 DONALD, David, ed. *Why the North Won the Civil War.* Baton Rouge, 1960. (Five essays, each exploring a different explanation.)†

15 EISENSCHIML, Otto and Ralph G. NEWMAN, eds. *The American Iliad: The Epic Story of the Civil War as Narrated by Eyewitnesses and Contemporaries.* Indianapolis, 1947.†

16 FISH, Carl R. *The American Civil War: An Interpretation,* ed. William E. Smith. New York, 1937.

1 FOOTE, Shelby. *The Civil War: A Narrative.* 2 vols. to date. New York, 1958-1963. (Largely a military account.)

2 GATES, Paul W. *Agriculture and the Civil War.* New York, 1965.

3 GREELEY, Horace. *The American Conflict.* 2 vols. Hartford, 1864-1866.

4 HANSEN, Harry. *The Civil War.* New York, 1961.†

5 HARWELL, Richard B., ed. *The Confederate Reader.* New York, 1957.

6 HARWELL, Richard B., ed. *The Union Reader.* New York, 1958.

7 HESSELTINE, William B. *Civil War Prisons: A Study in War Psychology.* Columbus, Ohio, 1930.

8 HESSELTINE, William B., ed. *The Tragic Conflict: The Civil War and Reconstruction.* New York, 1962.

9 LONN, Ella. *Desertion during the Civil War.* New York, 1928.

10 LURAGHI, Raimondo. *Stori della Guerra Civile Americana.* Turin, 1966. (A massive narrative, concentrating upon military history.)

11 MC MASTER, John B. *A History of the People of the United States during Lincoln's Administration.* New York, 1927.†

12 MC PHERSON, Edward, ed. *The Political History of the United States ... during the Great Rebellion.* 3d ed. Washington, D.C., 1876. (A valuable compilation of political documents.)

13 MC WHINEY, Grady, ed. *Grant, Lee, Lincoln and the Radicals: Essays on Civil War Leadership.* Evanston, Ill., 1964.†

14 MARX, Karl and Frederick ENGELS. *The Civil War in the United States,* ed. Richard Enmale. New York, 1937.†

15 MASSEY, Mary E. *Bonnet Brigades: American Woman and the Civil War.* New York, 1966.

16 MEREDITH, Roy. *Mr. Lincoln's Contemporaries: An Album of Portraits by Mathew B. Brady.* New York, 1951.

17 MIERS, Earl S. *The American Civil War.* New York, 1961. (A pictorial history.)

18 MIERS, Earl S. *The Great Rebellion: The Emergence of the American Conscience.* Cleveland, 1958.†

19 MILLER, Francis T., ed. *The Photographic History of the Civil War.* 10 vols. New York, 1911.

20 MILTON, George F. *Conflict: The American Civil War.* New York, 1941.

21 MOORE, Frank, ed. *The Rebellion Record: A Diary of American Events, with Documents, Narratives, Illustrative Incidents, Poetry, etc.* 12 vols. New York, 1862-1868.

22 NEVINS, Allan. *The War for the Union.* 2 vols. to date. New York, 1959-1960. (The most ambitious and successful modern scholarly history covering all phases of the conflict.)

23 NICHOLS, Roy F. "The Operation of American Democracy, 1861-1865: Some Questions." *J S Hist,* XXV (1959), 31-52.

24 NICHOLS, Roy F. *The Stakes of Power, 1847-1877.* New York, 1961.†

25 RANDALL, J. G. and David DONALD. *The Civil War and Reconstruction.* 2d ed. Boston, 1961. (The standard text, with extensive bibliographies.)

26 RANDALL, J. G. "The Civil War Restudied." *J S Hist,* VI (1940), 439-457.

27 RAWLEY, James A. *Turning Points of the Civil War.* Lincoln, Nebr., 1966.

28 RHODES, James F. *History of the Civil War, 1861-1865.* New York, 1917.

1 RHODES, James F. *History of the United States from the Compromise of 1850 [to the Final Restoration of Home Rule at the South.]* 7 vols. New York, 1893-1906. (Still the fullest scholarly history of the whole era, though largely superseded for the years 1861-1863 by Nevins' *War for the Union.*)†

2 RHODES, James F. *Lectures on the American Civil War.* New York, 1913.

3 SANDBURG, Carl. *Storm over the Land.* New York, 1942.

4 WARREN, Robert P. *The Legacy of the Civil War: Meditations on the Centennial.* New York, 1961.†

5 WILEY, Bell I. and Hirst D. MILHOLLEN. *They Who Fought Here.* New York, 1959. (A pictorial history, with elaborate accompanying text.)

6 WILSON, Edmund. *Patriotic Gore: Studies in the Literature of the American Civil War.* New York, 1962.†

VII. Military Studies

7 ADAMS, George W. *Doctors in Blue: The Medical History of the Union Army in the Civil War.* New York, 1952.†

8 AMANN, William F., ed. *Personnel of the Civil War.* 2 vols. New York, 1961.

9 BARRETT, John G. "The Confederate States of America at War on Land and Sea," in *Writing Southern History,* ed. Arthur S. Link and Rembert W. Patrick. Chapel Hill, 1965, pp. 273-294.†

10 BARRETT, John G. *Sherman's March Through the Carolinas.* Chapel Hill, 1956.

11 BIGELOW, John. *The Campaign of Chancellorsville: A Strategic and Tactical Study.* New Haven, 1910.

12 BRITTON, Wiley. *The Civil War on the Border: A Narrative of Operations in Missouri, Kansas, Arkansas, and the Indian Territory during the Years 1861-65.* 2 vols. New York, 1891-1899.

13 BROWN, Dee A. *The Bold Cavaliers: Morgan's 2nd Kentucky Cavalry Raiders.* Philadelphia, 1959.

14 BROWN, Dee A. *The Galvanized Yankees.* Urbana, 1963.

15 BROWN, Dee A. *Grierson's Raid.* Urbana, 1954.†

16 BROWNLEE, Richard S. *Gray Ghosts of the Confederacy: Guerilla Warfare in the West, 1861-1865.* Baton Rouge, 1958.

17 BUEL, Clarence C. and Robert U. JOHNSON, eds. *Battles and Leaders of the Civil War.* 4 vols. New York, 1887. (Important compilation of reminiscences by leading military men on both sides.)

18 BURNE, Alfred H. *Lee, Grant and Sherman: A Study in Leadership in 1864-65.* London, 1938.

19 *Campaigns of the Civil War.* 13 vols. New York, 1881-1883. (Monographs on the major campaigns, often by participants.)

20 CAPERS, Gerald M. *Occupied City: New Orleans under the Federals, 1862-1865.* Lexington, Ky., 1965.

1 CATTON, Bruce. *Glory Road: The Bloody Route from Fredericksburg to Gettysburg.* Garden City, N.Y., 1952. (The second volume in a series.)†

2 CATTON, Bruce. *Mr. Lincoln's Army.* Garden City, N.Y., 1951. (The first volume in a trilogy on the Army of the Potomac, combining magical style and superb research.)†

3 CATTON, Bruce. *A Stillness at Appomattox.* Garden City, N.Y., 1953. (The final, and probably the best, volume in the series on the Army of the Potomac.)†

4 CODDINGTON, Edwin B. *The Gettysburg Campaign.* New York, 1968.

5 COLTON, Ray C. *The Civil War in the Western Territories: Arizona, Colorado, New Mexico, and Utah.* Norman, Okla., 1959.

6 CONNELLY, Thomas L. *Army of the Heartland: The Army of Tennessee, 1861-1862.* Baton Rouge, 1967.

7 COX, Jacob D. *The Battle of Franklin, Tennessee, November 30, 1864.* New York, 1897.

8 COX, Jacob D. *The March to the Sea: Franklin and Nashville.* New York, 1882.

9 CUNLIFFE, Marcus. "The American Military Tradition," in H. C. Allen and C. P. Hill, eds., *British Essays in American History.* London, 1957, pp. 207-224.

10 CUNNINGHAM, Edward. *The Port Hudson Campaign, 1862-1863.* Baton Rouge, 1963.

11 CUNNINGHAM, H. H. *Doctors in Gray: The Confederate Medical Service.* Baton Rouge, 1958.

12 DAVIS, Burke. *To Appomattox: Nine April Days, 1865.* New York, 1959.†

13 DONALD, David. "The Confederate as a Fighting Man." *J S Hist,* XXV (1959), 178-193.

14 DORNBUSCH, Charles E., ed. *Regimental Publications & Personal Narratives of the Civil War.* 2 vols. to date. New York, 1961-1967. (An elaborate bibliography of unit histories and autobiographies, arranged by state.)

15 DOWDEY, Clifford. *Death of a Nation: The Story of Lee and His Men at Gettysburg.* New York, 1958.

16 DOWDEY, Clifford. *Lee's Last Campaign: The Story of Lee and His Men Against Grant.* Boston, 1960.

17 DOWDEY, Clifford. *The Seven Days: The Emergence of Lee.* Boston, 1964.

18 DOWNEY, Fairfax. *Clash of Cavalry: The Battle of Brandy Station, June 9, 1863.* New York, 1959.

19 DOWNEY, Fairfax. *Storming the Gateway: Chattanooga, 1863.* New York, 1960

20 DUKE, Basil W. *Morgan's Cavalry.* New York, 1906.

21 DUPUY, R. Ernest and Trevor N. DUPUY. *Military Heritage of America.* New York, 1956.

22 DYER, Frederick H. *A Compendium of the War of the Rebellion.* 3 vols. Des Moines, 1908.

23 EDWARDS, William B. *Civil War Guns.* Harrisburg, 1962.

24 ESPOSITO, Vincent J. *The West Point Atlas of the Civil War.* New York, 1962. (A superb collection of maps, indispensable to any understanding of the major battles.)

25 FALLS, Cyril. *A Hundred Years of War.* New York, 1954.

26 FOX, William F. *Regimental Losses in the American Civil War, 1861-1865.* Albany, 1889.

1 FREEMAN, Douglas S. and Grady MC WHINEY, eds. *Lee's Dispatches: Unpublished Letters of General Robert E. Lee, C.S.A., to Jefferson Davis and the War Department of the Confederate States of America, 1862-65.* New York, 1957.

2 FREEMAN, Douglas S. *Lee's Lieutenants: A Study in Command.* 3 vols. New York, 1942-1944. (Masterful portraits of Lee's principal subordinates.)

3 FREIDEL, Frank. "General Orders 100 and Military Government." *Miss Val Hist Rev,* XXXII (1946), 541-556. (Study of the basic rules of war followed by Union commanders.)

4 HALL, Martin H. *Sibley's New Mexico Campaign.* Austin, Tex., 1960.

5 HASSLER, Warren W., Jr. *Commanders of the Army of the Potomac.* Baton Rouge, 1962.

6 HASSLER, Warren W., Jr. "The First Day's Battle of Gettysburg." *C W Hist,* VI (1960), 259-276.

7 HAY, Thomas R. *Hood's Tennessee Campaign.* New York, 1929.

8 HAYDON, F. Stansbury. *Aeronautics in the Union and Confederate Armies.* Baltimore, 1941.

9 HENDERSON, G. F. R. *The Civil War, a Soldier's View: A Collection of Civil War Writings,* ed. Jay Luvaas. Chicago, 1958. (Essays by the British biographer of "Stonewall" Jackson.)

10 HORN, Stanley F. *The Army of Tennessee.* 2d ed. Norman, Okla., 1953.

11 HORN, Stanley F. *The Decisive Battle of Nashville.* Baton Rouge, 1956.

12 HUNT, Aurora. *The Army of the Pacific: Its Operations in California, Texas, Arizona, New Mexico, Utah, Nevada, Oregon, Washington, Plains Region, Mexico, Etc., 1860-1866.* Glendale, Calif., 1951.

13 JONES, Archer. *Confederate Strategy from Shiloh to Vicksburg.* Baton Rouge, 1961.

14 JOHNSON, Ludwell H. *Red River Campaign: Politics and Cotton in the Civil War.* Baltimore, 1958.

15 JOHNSTON, Angus J., II. *Virginia Railroads in the Civil War.* Chapel Hill, 1961.

16 JOHNSTON, Robert M. *Bull Run: Its Strategy and Tactics.* New York, 1913.

17 LEACH, Jack F. *Conscription in the United States: Historical Background.* Rutland, 1952.

18 LIVERMORE, Thomas L. *Numbers and Losses in the Civil War in America, 1861-1865.* Boston, 1901.

19 LONN, Ella. *Foreigners in the Union Army and Navy.* Baton Rouge, 1951.

20 LORD, Francis A. *They Fought for the Union.* Harrisburg, 1960.

21 LUVAAS, Jay. *The Military Legacy of the Civil War: The European Inheritance.* Chicago, 1959. (The impact of the Civil War on European military thinking.)

22 MC WHINEY, Grady. "Controversy in Kentucky: Braxton Bragg's Campaign of 1862." *C W Hist,* VI (1960), 5-42.

23 MC WHINEY, Grady. "Who Whipped Whom? Confederate Defeat Re-examined." *C W Hist,* XI (1965), 5-26.

24 MAURICE, Frederick. *Statemen and Soldiers of the Civil War: A Study of the Conduct of War.* Boston, 1926.

25 MAXWELL, William Q. *Lincoln's Fifth Wheel: The Political History of the United States Sanitary Commission.* New York, 1956.

1 MENEELY, A. H. *The War Department, 1861.* New York, 1928. (Invaluable study of the disorganization and corruption in the Union war office at the beginning of the conflict.)

2 MIERS, Earl S., *Web of Victory: Grant at Vicksburg.* New York, 1955.

3 MIERS, Earl S. and Richard B. BROWN. *Gettysburg.* New Brunswick, N.J., 1948. (Ninety-two excerpts from contemporary accounts.)†

4 MONAGHAN, Jay. *Civil War on the Western Border, 1854-1865.* Boston, 1955.

5 MONTGOMERY, James S. *The Shaping of a Battle: Gettysburg.* Philadelphia, 1959.

6 NAISAWALD, L. Van Loan. *Grape and Cannister: The Story of the Field Artillery of the Army of the Potomac, 1861-1865.* New York, 1960.

7 NICHOLS, James J. *The Confederate Quartermaster in the Trans-Mississippi.* Austin, Tex., 1964.

8 NOLAN, Alan T. *The Iron Brigade: A Military History.* New York, 1961.

9 NYE, Wilbur S. *Here Come the Rebels!* Baton Rouge, 1965. (The Gettysburg campaign.)

10 OATES, Stephen B. *Confederate Cavalry West of the River.* Austin, Tex., 1961.

11 ORLEANS, Louis Phillippe Albert d', comte de Paris. *History of the Civil War in America.* 4 vols. Philadelphia, 1875-1888.

12 PATRICK, Rembert W. *The Fall of Richmond.* Baton Rouge, 1960.

13 PULLEN, John J. *The Twentieth Maine: A Volunteer Regiment in the Civil War.* Philadelphia, 1957.†

14 ROBERTSON, James I., Jr. *The Stonewall Brigade.* Baton Rouge, 1963.

15 ROPES, John C. and W. R. LIVERMORE. *The Story of the Civil War.* 4 vols. New York, 1894-1913. (Still one of the most comprehensive and useful military narratives.)

16 SHANNON, Fred A. *The Organization and Administration of the Union Army, 1861-1865.* 2 vols. Cleveland, 1928. (Masterful, sardonic analysis of the incompetence which reigned in the Federal forces.)

17 SMITH, George W. *Medicines for the Union Army: The United States Army Laboratories during the Civil War.* Madison, Wis., 1962.

18 SPARKS, David S. "General Patrick's Progress: Intelligence and Security in the Army of the Potomac." *C W Hist,* X (1964), 371-384.

19 STACKPOLE, Edward J. *Chancelorsville: Lee's Greatest Battle.* Harrisburg, 1958.

20 STACKPOLE, Edward J. *From Cedar Mountain to Antietam: August-September, 1862.* Harrisburg, 1959.

21 STACKPOLE, Edward J. *Sheridan in the Shenandoah: Jubal Early's Nemesis.* Harrisburg, 1961.

22 STACKPOLE, Edward J. *They Met at Gettysburg.* Harrisburg, 1956.

23 STEELE, Matthew F. *American Campaigns.* 2 vols. Washington, D.C., 1909. (The second volume is a useful compilation of battle maps.)

24 STERN, Philip Van Doren. *An End to Valor: The Last Days of the Civil War.* Boston, 1958.

25 STEWART, George R. *Pickett's Charge: A Microhistory of the Final Attack at Gettysburg, July 3, 1863.* Boston, 1959.

1 TUCKER, Glenn. *Chickamauga: Bloody Battle in the West.* Indianapolis, 1961.

2 TUCKER, Glenn. *High Tide at Gettysburg: The Campaign in Pennsylvania.* Indianapolis, 1958.†

3 TUCKER, Glenn. *Lee and Longstreet at Gettysburg.* Indianapolis, 1968.

4 TURNER, George E. *Victory Rode the Rails.* Indianapolis, 1953. (How both Union and Confederate commanders used the railroads.)

5 UPTON, Emory. *The Military Policy of the United States.* Washington, D.C., 1904.

6 VANDIVER, Frank E. *Rebel Brass: The Confederate Command System.* Baton Rouge, 1956.

7 WALKER, Peter F. *Vicksburg: A People at War, 1860-1865.* Chapel Hill, 1960.

8 *War of the Rebellion: . . . Official Records of the Union and Confederate Armies.* 128 vols. Washington, D.C., 1880-1901. (A vast compilation of despatches, battle reports, telegrams, and other military correspondence.)

9 WARNER, Ezra J. *Generals in Blue: Lives of the Union Commanders.* Baton Rouge, 1964. (Excellent brief biographies.)

10 WARNER, Ezra J. *Generals in Gray: Lives of the Confederate Commanders.* Baton Rouge, 1959.

11 WASSON, R. Gordon. *The Hall Carbine Affair: A Study in Contemporary Folklore.* New York, 1948. (Dispels the legend that J. P. Morgan was behind Union ordnance scandals.)

12 WEIGLEY, Russell F. *Towards an American Army: Military Thought from Washington to Marshall.* New York, 1962.

13 WILEY, Bell I. *The Life of Billy Yank: The Common Soldier of the Union.* Indianapolis, 1952. (Vivid account of the ideas and actions of the Union soldiers.)†

14 WILEY, Bell I. *The Life of Johnny Reb: The Common Soldier of the Confederacy.* Indianapolis, 1943. (A work parallel to the one just cited, and of equal merit; both are basic books.)†

15 WILLIAMS, Kenneth P. *Lincoln Finds a General: A Military Study of the Civil War.* 5 vols. New York, 1949-1959. (The most thorough modern study of the Union armies, unfortunately left incomplete at the author's death.)

16 WILLIAMS, T. Harry. "The Attack upon West Point during the Civil War." *Miss Val Hist Rev,* XXV (1939), 491-504.

17 WILLIAMS, T. Harry. *McClellan, Sherman and Grant.* New Brunswick, N.J., 1962.

18 WISE, Jennings C. *The Long Arm of Lee: Or the History of the Artillery of the Army of Northern Virginia.* 2 vols. Lynchburg, 1915.

19 WOLSELEY, Field Marshall Viscount. *The American Civil War: An English View,* ed. James A. Rawley. Charlottesville, 1965.

20 WOOD, W. Birkbeck and J. E. EDMONDS. *A History of the Civil War in the United States, 1861-65.* London, 1905.†

21 WRIGHT, Edward N. *Conscientious Objectors in the Civil War.* Philadelphia, 1931.†

See also **5**.16, **6**.4, **6**.7, **7**.4, **7**.5, **8**.5, **8**.6, **8**.7, **8**.8, **8**.9, **10**.3, **10**.9, **10**.10, **11**.16, **11**.17, **12**.1, **12**.2, **12**.10, **12**.11, **13**.10, **13**.11, **14**.2, **14**.3, **14**.7, **14**.12, **15**.1, **15**.2, **15**.3, **15**.6, **15**.7, **15**.8, **15**.9, **15**.11, **15**.12, **16**.5, **16**.7, **16**.8, **16**.9, **17**.1, **17**.7, **18**.1, **18**.2, **18**.7, **18**.8, **18**.9, **18**.10 **18**.11, **18**.12, **19**.1, **19**.4, **19**.5, **19**.6, **19**.17, **19**.18, **20**.1, **20**.2, **20**.7, **20**.9, **20**.10, **20**.11, **20**.12, **20**.13, **20**.14, **20**.15, **21**.3, **21**.12, **23**.16, **24**.2, **24**.3, **24**.4, **24**.5, **24**.6, **24**.7, **24**.11, **24**.12, **24**.13, **24**.14, **25**.3, **25**.8, **25**.9, **25**.10, **25**.11, **26**.1, **26**.6, **26**.7, **27**.1,

27.2, **27**.8, **27**.9, **28**.4, **28**.5, **28**.9, **28**.10, **29**.4, **29**.5, **30**.1, **30**.4, **30**.5, **30**.8, **30**.10, **31**.10, **31**.11, **32**.1, **32**.2, **32**.3, **32**.4, **32**.5, **32**.6, **32**.7, **32**.11, **32**.12, **33**.4, **33**.5, **33**.6, **33**.7, **34**.4, **34**.5, **34**.11, **34**.12, **34**.13, **35**.12, **36**.2, **36**.8, **36**.9, **36**.10, **36**.11.

VIII. The War at Sea

1 AMMEN, Daniel. *The Atlantic Coast.* New York, 1883.

2 ANDERSON, Bern. *By Sea and By River: The Naval History of the Civil War.* New York, 1962.

3 BAXTER, James P., III. *The Introduction of the Ironclad Warship.* Cambridge, Mass., 1933.

4 BOYER, Samuel P. *Naval Surgeon: Blockading the South, 1862-1866,* ed. Elinor and James A. Barnes. Bloomington, 1963.

5 BOYNTON, Charles B. *The History of the Navy during the Rebellion.* 2 vols. New York, 1867-1868.

6 DALY, R. W. *How the Merrimac Won: The Strategic Story of the C.S.S. Virginia.* New York, 1957.

7 DALZELL, George W. *The Flight from the Flag: The Continuing Effect of the Civil War upon the American Carrying Trade.* Chapel Hill, 1940.

8 GOSNELL, H. Allen. *Guns on the Western Waters: The Story of River Gunboats in the Civil War.* Baton Rouge, 1949.

9 HANNA, Kathryn A. "Incidents of the Confederate Blockade." *J S Hist,* XI (1945), 214-229.

10 HOOLE, William S. *Four Years in the Confederate Navy: The Career of Captain John Low on the C.S.S. Fingal, Florida, Alabama, Tuscaloosa, and Ajax.* Athens, Ga., 1964.

11 JONES, Virgil C. *The Civil War at Sea.* 3 vols. New York, 1960-1962. (The most complete modern account, largely narrative.)

12 LONG, John S. "Glory Hunting Off Havana: Wilkes and the *Trent* Affair." *C W Hist,* IX (1963), 133-144.

13 MACARTNEY, Clarence E. *Mr. Lincoln's Admirals.* New York, 1956.

14 MC CORDOCK, Robert S. *The Yankee Cheese Box.* Philadelphia, 1938. (The *U.S.S. Monitor.*)

15 MAHAN, Alfred T. *The Gulf and Inland Waters.* New York, 1883.

16 MERRILL, James M. *The Rebel Shore: The Story of Union Sea Power in the Civil War.* Boston, 1957.

17 MILLIGAN, John D. *Gunboats down the Mississippi.* Annapolis, 1965.

18 *Official Records of the Union and Confederate Navies in the War of the Rebellion.* 30 vols. Washington, D.C., 1894-1922. (The authorized compilation of official reports, despatches, correspondence, etc.)

19 OWSLEY, Frank L., Jr. *The C.S.S. Florida: Her Building and Operations.* Philadelphia, 1965.

20 PAULLIN, Charles O. "President Lincoln and the Navy." *Am Hist Rev,* XIV (1909), 284-303.

21 PERRY, Milton F. *Infernal Machines: The Story of Confederate Submarine and Mine Warfare.* Baton Rouge, 1965.

22 ROBINSON, William M., Jr. *The Confederate Privateers.* New Haven, 1928.

1 ROBINTON, Madeline R. *An Introduction to the Papers of the New York Prize Court, 1861-1865.* New York, 1945.

2 SCHARF, J. T. *History of the Confederate Navy.* New York, 1887.

3 SOLEY, James R. *The Blockade and the Cruisers.* New York, 1883.

4 STILL, William N., Jr. "Confederate Naval Strategy: The Ironclad." *J S Hist,* XXVII (1961), 330-343.

5 STILL, William N., Jr. "Facilities for the Construction of War Vessels in the Confederacy." *J S Hist,* XXXI (1965), 285-304.

6 SUMMERSELL, Charles G. *The Cruise of C.S.S. Sumter.* Tuscaloosa, 1965.

7 TREXLER, Harrison A. *The Confederate Ironclad 'Virginia' ('Merrimac').* Chicago, 1938.

8 VANDIVER, Frank E., ed. *Confederate Blockade Running through Bermuda, 1861-1865: Letters and Cargo Manifests.* Austin, Tex., 1947.

9 WEST, Richard S., Jr. *Mr. Lincoln's Navy.* New York, 1957.

10 WHITE, William C. and Ruth WHITE. *Tin Can on a Shingle.* New York, 1957.

See also 12.12, 12.13, 13.5, 14.1, 25.4, 25 .7, 28.6, 28.7, 28.8, 31.1, 31.2, 31.3, 37.6, 37.7, 37.8, 37.11.

IX. Politics in the North: National, State, and Local Studies

11 ADAMSON, Hans C. *Rebellion in Missouri, 1861: Nathaniel Lyon and His Army of the West.* Philadelphia, 1961.

12 AMBLER, Charles H. *A History of West Virginia.* New York, 1933.

13 BENNETT, Royal A. *All Quiet on the Yamhill: The Civil War in Oregon,* ed. Gunter Barth. Eugene, 1959.

14 BENTON, Josiah H. *Voting in the Field: A Forgotten Chapter of the Civil War.* Boston, 1915. (The standard study of soldier voting.)

15 BOGUE, Allan G. "Bloc and Party in the United States Senate, 1861-1863." *C W Hist,* XIII (1967), 221-241.

16 BOYKIN, Edward C. *Congress and the Civil War.* New York, 1955.

17 BRADLEY, Erwin S. *The Triumph of Militant Republicanism: A Study of Pennsylvania and Presidential Politics, 1860-1872.* Philadelphia, 1964.

18 BRUMMER, Sidney D. *Political History of New York State during the Period of the Civil War.* New York, 1911.

19 CARLETON, William G. "Civil War Dissidence in the North: The Perspective of a Century." *S Atl Q,* LXV (1966), 390-402.

20 CARTER, John D. "Abraham Lincoln and the California Patronage." *Am Hist Rev,* XLVIII (1943), 495-506.

21 CASTEL, Albert. *A Frontier State at War: Kansas, 1861-1865.* Ithaca, 1958.

22 CLARK, Charles B. "Politics in Maryland during the Civil War." *Md Hist Mag,* XXXVI (1941), 239-262, 381-393; XXXVII (1942), 171-192, 378-399; XXXVIII (1943), 230-260; XXXIX (1944), 149-161, 315-331; XL (1945), 233-241, 295-309; XLI (1946), 132-158.

1 CLARK, Charles B. "Suppression and Control of Maryland, 1861-1865: A Study of Federal-State Relations during Civil Conflict." *Md Hist Mag,* LIV (1959), 241-271.

2 CLARK, O. B. *Politics of Iowa during the Civil War and Reconstruction.* Iowa City, 1911.

3 COLE, Arthur C. *The Era of the Civil War, 1848-1870 (The Centennial History of Illinois,* III). Springfield, Ill., 1919.

4 CRENSHAW, Ollinger. "The Knights of the Golden Circle: The Career of George Bickley." *Am Hist Rev,* XLVII (1941), 23-50.

5 CROSS, Jasper W., Jr. "The Civil War Comes to Egypt [Southern Illinois]," *J Ill State Hist Soc,* XLIV (1951), 160-169.

6 CURRY, Leonard P. *Blueprint for Modern America: Nonmilitary Legislation of the First Civil War Congress.* Nashville, 1968.

7 CURRY, Leonard P. "Congressional Democrats, 1861-1863." *C W Hist,* XII (1966), 213-229.

8 CURRY, Richard O. *A House Divided: A Study of Statehood Politics and the Copperhead Movement in West Virginia.* Pittsburgh, 1964.

9 CURRY, Richard O. "The Union as It Was: A Critique of Recent Interpretations of the Copperheads." *C W Hist,* XIII (1967), 25-39.

10 DAVIS, Stanton L. *Pennsylvania Politics, 1860-1863.* Cleveland, 1935.

11 DUDLEY, Harold M. "The Election of 1864." *Miss Val Hist Rev,* XVIII (1932), 500-518.

12 DUSINBERRE, William. *Civil War Issues in Philadelphia, 1856-1865.* Philadelphia, 1965.

13 FLICK, Alexander C., ed. *History of the State of New York,* VII. New York, 1935. (Contains two chapters on New York state during the war and Reconstruction period.)

14 GAMBILL, Edward L. "Who Were the Senate Radicals?" *C W Hist,* XI (1965), 237-244.

15 GLONECK, James F. "Lincoln, Johnson, and the Baltimore Ticket," *A Lincoln Q,* VI (1951), 255-271.

16 GRAY, Wood. *The Hidden Civil War: The Story of the Copperheads.* New York, 1942.†

17 GREEN, Constance M. *Washington: Village and Capital, 1800-1878.* Princeton, 1962.

18 HANCOCK, Harold B. *Delaware during the Civil War: A Political History.* Wilmington, Del., 1961.

19 HARBISON, Winfred A. "Indiana Republicans and the Re-election of President Lincoln." *Ind Mag Hist,* XXXIV (1938), 42-64.

20 HARBISON, Winfred A. "Lincoln and the Indiana Republicans, 1861-62." *Ind Mag Hist,* XXXIII (1937), 277-303.

21 HICKEN, Victor. *Illinois in the Civil War.* Urbana, 1966.

22 HUBBART, H. C. *The Older Middle West, 1840-1880: Its Social, Economic and Political Life and Sectional Tendencies Before, During and After the Civil War.* New York, 1936.

23 JONES, Robert H. *The Civil War in the Northwest: Nebraska, Wisconsin, Iowa, Minnesota, and the Dakotas.* Norman, Okla., 1960.

24 JONES, Stanley L. "Agrarian Radicalism in Illinois' Constitutional Convention of 1862." *J Ill State Hist Soc,* XLVIII (1955), 271-282.

25 KIRKLAND, Edward C. *The Peacemakers of 1864.* New York, 1927.

1 KLEMENT, Frank L. "Clement L. Vallandigham's Exile in the Confederacy, May 25-June 17, 1863." *J S Hist,* XXXI (1965), 149-163.

2 KLEMENT, Frank L. *The Copperheads in the Middle West.* Chicago, 1960. (The standard work.)

3 KLEMENT, Frank L. *Wisconsin and the Civil War.* Madison, Wis., 1963.

4 KNAPP, Charles M. *New Jersey Politics during the Period of the Civil War and Reconstruction.* New York, 1924.

5 LAUGHLIN, Sceva B. *Missouri Politics during the Civil War.* Salem, Ore., 1930.

6 LEECH, Margaret. *Reveille in Washington.* New York, 1941. (A spirited account of politics and life in the capital during the war.)†

7 LINDEN, Glenn M. "'Radicals' and Economic Policies: The House of Representatives, 1861-1873." *C W Hist,* XIII (1967), 51-65.

8 LINDEN, Glenn M. "'Radicals' and Economic Policies: The Senate, 1861-1873." *J S Hist,* XXXII (1966), 189-199.

9 LUTHIN, Reinhard H. "A Discordant Chapter in Lincoln's Administration: The Davis-Blair Controversy." *Md Hist Mag,* XXXIX (1944), 25-48.

10 MAC KAY, Winnifred. "Philadelphia during the Civil War, 1861-1865." *Penn Mag Hist and Biog,* LXX (1946), 3-51.

11 MALLAM, William D. "Lincoln and the Conservatives." *J S Hist,* XXVIII (1962), 31-45.

12 NEVINS, Allan. *The Statesmanship of the Civil War.* New York, 1953.

13 NIVEN, John. *Connecticut for the Union: The Role of the State in the Civil War.* New Haven, 1965.

14 PARRISH, William E. *Turbulent Partnership: Missouri and the Union, 1861-1865.* Columbia, Mo., 1963.

15 PIERSON, William W., Jr. "The Committee on the Conduct of the Civil War." *Am Hist Rev,* XXIII (1918), 550-576.

16 PORTER, George H. *Ohio Politics during the Civil War Period.* New York, 1911.

17 PRATT, Harry E. "The Repudiation of Lincoln's War Policy in 1862–Stuart-Swett Congressional Campaign." *J Ill State Hist Soc,* XXIV (1931), 129-140.

18 ROSEBOOM, Eugene H. *The Civil War Era, 1850-1873 (The History of the State of Ohio,* IV). Columbus, Ohio, 1944.

19 ROSEBOOM, Eugene H. "Southern Ohio and the Union in 1863." *Miss Val Hist Rev,* XXXIX (1952), 29-44.

20 SIMON, John Y. "The Politics of the Morrill Act." *Ag Hist,* XXXVII (1963), 103-111.

21 SPRAGUE, Dean. *Freedom under Lincoln.* Boston, 1965. (An account of the restraints upon civil rights imposed by the Union government.)

22 STAMPP, Kenneth M. *Indiana Politics during the Civil War.* Indianapolis, 1949. (A model study.)

23 STAMPP, Kenneth M. "The Milligan Case and the Election of 1864 in Indiana." *Miss Val Hist Rev,* XXXI (1944), 41-58.

24 STUTLER, Boyd B. *West Virginia in the Civil War.* Charleston, W.Va., 1963.

25 THORNBROUGH, Emma L. *Indiana in the Civil War Era, 1850-1880.* Indianapolis, 1965.

26 TOWNSEND, William H. *Lincoln and the Bluegrass: Slavery and Civil War in Kentucky.* Lexington, Ky., 1955.

1 TREFOUSSE, Hans L. "The Joint Committee on the Conduct of the War: A Reassessment." *C W Hist,* X (1964), 5-19.

2 VAN RIPER, Paul P. and Keith A. SUTHERLAND. "The Northern Civil Service, 1861-1865." *C W Hist,* XI (1965), 351-369.

3 WAINWRIGHT, Nicholas B. "The Loyal Opposition in Civil War Philadelphia." *Penn Mag Hist and Biog,* LXXXVIII (1964), 294-315.

4 WARE, Edith E. *Political Opinion in Massachusetts during the Civil War and Reconstruction.* New York, 1916.

5 WEEDEN, William B. *War Government, Federal and State, in Massachusetts, New York, Pennsylvania, and Indiana.* Boston, 1906.

6 WILLIAMS, T. Harry. "Voters in Blue: The Citizen Soldiers of the Civil War." *Miss Val Hist Rev,* XXXI (1944), 187-204.

7 WINTHER, Oscar O. "The Soldier Vote in the Election of 1864." *N Y Hist,* XXV (1944), 440-458.

See also **6.1, 6.5, 6.6, 7.1, 7.3, 7.7, 7.8, 8.5, 8.7, 8.8, 8.10, 8.13, 8.14, 9.1, 9.2, 9.4, 9.5, 9.6, 10.4, 10.5, 11.5, 13.6, 13.7, 15.13, 15.15, 16.2, 16.3, 16.4, 16.6, 17.2, 17.3, 17.12, 20.4, 20.5, 20.6, 21.2, 21.5, 21.7, 21.13, 21.16, 21.18, 22.2, 22.3, 22.5, 22.15, 22.19, 23.3, 23.8, 23.13, 23.17, 23.21, 24.8, 26.5, 26.8, 26.9, 27.11, 27.12, 31.5, 31.6, 31.7, 31.8, 31.9, 33.4, 33.5, 33.6, 33.7, 33.15, 33.16, 33.17, 34.1, 34.2, 34.6, 34.7, 34.8, 35.9, 35.10, 35.13, 36.1, 36.6, 36.7, 37.4, 37.5, 37.6, 37.8, 38.3.**

X. The Wartime Union: Economic, Social, and Intellectual Aspects

8 ANDREANO, Ralph, ed. *The Economic Impact of the American Civil War.* Cambridge, Mass., 1962.†

9 ANDREWS, J. Cutler. *The North Reports the Civil War.* Pittsburgh, 1955. (The comprehensive history of wartime journalism.)

10 BAXTER, Maurice G. "Encouragement of Immigration to the Middle West during the Era of the Civil War." *Ind Mag Hist,* XLVI (1950), 25-38.

11 COCHRAN, Thomas C. "Did the Civil War Retard Industrialization?" *Miss Val Hist Rev,* XLVIII (1961), 197-210. (A basic article, challenging the conventional stereotype.)

12 COULTER, E. Merton. "Effects of Secession upon the Commerce of the Mississippi Valley." *Miss Val Hist Rev,* III (1916), 275-300.

13 CROZIER, Emmet. *Yankee Reporters, 1861-65.* New York, 1956.

14 ENGERMAN, Stanley L. "The Economic Impact of the Civil War." *Explorations in Entrepreneurial Hist,* 2d ser., III (1966), 176-199.

15 ERICKSON, Charlotte. *American Industry and the European Immigrant, 1860-1885.* Cambridge, Mass., 1957.

16 FARNHAM, Wallace D. "'The Weakened Spring of Government': A Study in Nineteenth-Century American History." *Am Hist Rev,* LXVIII (1963), 662-680. (A study of the government's role in the building of the Union Pacific Railroad.)

17 FISH, Carl R. "The Northern Railroads, April, 1861." *Am Hist Rev,* XXII (1917), 778-793.

18 FISH, Carl R. "Social Relief in the Northwest during the Civil War." *Am Hist Rev,* XXII (1917), 309-324.

19 FITE, Emerson D. *Social and Industrial Conditions in the North during the Civil War.* New York, 1910. (Still the standard work.)

1 FOGEL, Robert W. *The Union Pacific Railroad: A Case in Premature Enterprise.* Baltimore, 1960.

2 FREDRICKSON, George M. *The Inner Civil War: Northern Intellectuals and the Crisis of the Union.* New York, 1965.

3 FREIDEL, Frank. "The Loyal Publication Society: A Pro-Union Propaganda Agency." *Miss Val Hist Rev,* XXVI (1939), 359-376.

4 FREIDEL, Frank, ed. *Union Pamphlets of the Civil War.* 2 vols. Cambridge, Mass., 1967. (Fifty-two contemporary pamphlets, superbly edited, giving an excellent sampling of the controversial literature of the period.)

5 FRIEDMAN, Milton. "Price, Income, and Monetary Changes in Three Wartime Periods." *Am Econ Rev,* XLII (1952), 612-625.

6 GATES, Paul W. "The Homestead Law in an Incongruous Land System." *Am Hist Rev,* XLI (1936), 652-681.

7 GILCHRIST, David T. and W. David LEWIS, eds. *Economic Change in the Civil War Era.* Greenville, Del., 1965.

8 HAMMOND, Bray. "The North's Empty Purse." *Am Hist Rev,* LXVII (1961), 1-18. (The dilemmas of the Union Treasury Department at the outbreak of war.)

9 JOHNSON, Ludwell. "The Butler Expedition of 1861-1862: The Profitable Side of War." *C W Hist,* XI (1965), 229-236.

10 JOHNSON, Ludwell H. "Commerce Between Northeastern Ports and the Confederacy, 1861-1865." *J Am Hist,* LIV (1967), 30-42.

11 JOHNSON, Ludwell H. "Contraband Trade during the Last Year of the Civil War." *Miss Val Hist Rev,* XLIX (1963), 635-652.

12 JOHNSON, Ludwell H. "Northern Profit and Profiteers: The Cotton Rings of 1864-1865." *C W Hist,* XII (1966), 101-115.

13 LUTHIN, Reinhard H. "Abraham Lincoln and the Tariff." *Am Hist Rev,* XLIX (1944), 609-629.

14 MC CAGUE, James. *Moguls and Iron Men: The Story of the First Transcontinental Railroad.* New York, 1964.

15 MAN, Albon P., Jr. "Labor Competition and the New York Draft Riots of 1863." *J Neg Hist,* XXXVI (1951), 375-405.

16 MERK, Frederick. *Economic History of Wisconsin during the Civil War Decade.* Madison, Wis., 1916.

17 MITCHELL, Wesley C. *A History of the Greenbacks, with Special Reference to the Economic Consequences of Their Issue, 1862-65.* Chicago, 1903.

18 MURPHEY, Hermon K. "The Northern Railroads and the Civil War." *Miss Val Hist Rev,* V (1918), 324-338.

19 RANDALL, J. G. "The Newspaper Problem . . . during the Civil War." *Am Hist Rev,* XXIII (1918), 303-323.

20 RATNER, Sidney. *American Taxation: Its History as a Social Force in Democracy.* New York, 1942. (The standard work.)

21 REIN, Bert W. *An Analysis and Critique of the Union Financing of the Civil War.* Amherst, 1962.†

22 RIEGEL, R. E. "Federal Operation of Southern Railroads during the Civil War." *Miss Val Hist Rev,* IX (1922), 126-138.

23 ROBERTS, A. Sellew. "The Federal Government and Confederate Cotton." *Am Hist Rev,* XXXIII (1927), 262-275.

1 ROBINSON, Marshall A. "Federal Debt Management: Civil War, World War I, and World War II'" *Am Econ Rev,* XLV (1955), 388-401.

2 SCHEIBER, Harry N. "Economic Change in the Civil War Era: An Analysis of Recent Studies." *C W Hist,* XI (1965), 396-411.

3 SHAPIRO, Henry D. *Confiscation of Confederate Property in the North.* Ithaca, 1962.†

4 SMITH, George W. "Broadsides for Freedom: Civil War Propaganda in New England." *N Eng Q,* XXI (1948), 291-312.

5 SMITH, George W. and Charles JUDAH, eds. *Life in the North during the Civil War: A Source History.* Albuquerque, 1966. (An invaluable documentary collection.)

6 SMITH, George W. "The National War Committee of the Citizens of New York." *N Y Hist,* XXVIII (1947), 440-457.

7 SMITH, George W. "Some Northern Wartime Attitudes toward the Post-Civil War South." *J S Hist,* X (1944), 253-274.

8 SMITH, Harry E. *The United States Federal Internal Tax History from 1861 to 1871.* Cambridge, Mass., 1914.

9 STARR, Louis M. *Bohemian Brigade: Civil War Newsmen in Action.* New York, 1954.†

10 STUDENSKI, Paul and Herman E. KROOS. *Financial History of the United States.* New York, 1952. (An excellent general survey, with chapters on wartime finance.)

11 SUMMERS, Festus P. *The Baltimore and Ohio in the Civil War.* New York, 1939.

12 SWEET, William W. *The Methodist Episcopal Church and the Civil War.* Cincinnati, 1912.

13 TAYLOR, George R. and Irene D. NEU. *The American Railroad Network, 1861-1890.* Cambridge, Mass., 1956.

14 VARTANIAN, Pershing. "The Cochran Thesis: A Critique in Statistical Analysis." *J Am Hist,* LI (1964), 77-89.

15 WARE, Norman J. *The Labor Movement in the United States, 1860-1895.* New York, 1929.†

16 WEBER, Thomas. *The Northern Railroads in the Civil War, 1861-1865.* New York, 1952.

17 WEISBERGER, Bernard A. *Reporters for the Union.* Boston, 1953.

18 WILLIAMS, Lorraine A. "Northern Intellectual Attitudes towards Lincoln, 1860-1865." *J Ill State Hist Soc,* LVII (1964), 270-283.

19 WILLIAMS, Lorraine A. "Northern Intellectual Reaction to Military Rule during the Civil War." *Historian,* XXVII (1965), 334-349.

See also **10**.1 **10**.2, **25**.1, **30**.9, **34**.3.

XI. History and Politics of the Confederacy: National, State, and Local Studies

20 ALEXANDER, Thomas B. "Persistent Whiggery in the Confederate South, 1860-1877." *J S Hist,* XXVII (1961), 305-329.

21 AMBROSE, Stephen E. "Yeoman Discontent in the Confederacy." *C W Hist,* VIII (1962), 259-268.

1 BAILEY, Hugh C. "Disaffection in the Alabama Hill Country, 1861." *C W Hist,* IV (1958), 183-194.

2 BAILEY, Hugh C. "Disloyalty in Early Confederate Alabama." *J S Hist,* XXIII (1957), 522-528.

3 BARRETT, John G. *The Civil War in North Carolina.* Chapel Hill, 1963.

4 BEARSS, Edwin C. *Decision in Mississippi: Mississippi's Important Role in the War between the States.* Jackson, Miss., 1962.

5 BETTERSWORTH, John K. *Confederate Mississippi: The People and Politics of a Cotton State in Wartime.* Baton Rouge, 1943.

6 BETTERSWORTH, John K. and James W. SILVER, eds. *Mississippi in the Confederacy.* 2 vols. Baton Rouge, 1961.

7 BILL, Alfred H. *The Beleaguered City: Richmond, 1861-1865.* New York, 1946.

8 BRAGG, Jefferson D. *Louisiana in the Confederacy.* Baton Rouge, 1941.

9 BUCHANAN, Lamont. *A Pictorial History of the Confederacy.* New York, 1951.

10 BRYAN, T. Conn. *Confederate Georgia.* Athens, Ga., 1953.

11 CAUTHEN, Charles E. *South Carolina Goes to War, 1861-1865.* Chapel Hill, 1950.†

12 COMMAGER, Henry S., ed. *The Defeat of the Confederacy: A Documentary Survey.* Princeton, 1964.†

13 COULTER, E. Merton. *The Civil War and Readjustment in Kentucky.* Chapel Hill, 1926.

14 COULTER, E. Merton. *The Confederate States of America, 1861-1865.* Baton Rouge, 1950. (A comprehensive history, strongest on social and economic conditions.)

15 CURRY, Jabez L. M. *Civil History of the Government of the Confederate States with Some Personal Reminiscences.* Richmond, 1901.

16 DAVIS, Jefferson. *The Rise and Fall of the Confederate Government.* 2 vols. New York, 1881. (A defense, by the President of the Confederate States of America.)†

17 DOWDY, Clifford. *The Land They Fought For.* Garden City, N.Y., 1955.

18 EATON, Clement. *A History of the Southern Confederacy.* New York, 1954. (The best survey.)†

19 FREEMAN, Douglas S. *The South To Posterity: An Introduction to the Writing of Confederate History.* New York, 1939.

20 GIPSON, Lawrence H. "The Collapse of the Confederacy." *Miss Val Hist Rev,* IV (1918), 437-458.

21 HENDRICK, Burton J. *Statesmen of the Lost Cause: Jefferson Davis and His Cabinet.* Boston, 1939.

22 HENRY, Robert S. *The Story of the Confederacy.* Indianapolis, 1931.

23 JOHNS, John E. *Florida During the Civil War.* Gainesville, 1963.

24 KIRWAN, Albert D., ed. *The Confederacy.* New York, 1959. (An admirable anthology, strong on social and economic changes.)†

25 KLINGBERG, Frank W. *The Southern Claims Commission.* Berkeley, 1955. (This federal agency after the war received thousands of claims from southerners who asserted they had always been loyal to the Union.)†

1 LAWRENCE, Alexander A. *A Present for Mr. Lincoln: The Story of Savannah from Secession to Sherman.* Macon, 1961.

2 LEE, Charles R., Jr. *The Confederate Constitutions.* Chapel Hill, 1963. (The standard work.)

3 LESLIE, William R. "The Confederate Constitution." *Mich Q Rev,* II (1963), 153-165.

4 MARTIN, Bessie. *Desertion of Alabama Troops from the Confederate Army: A Study in Sectionalism.* New York, 1932.

5 MASSEY, Mary E. "The Confederate States of America: The Homefront," in *Writing Southern History,* ed. Arthur S. Link and Rembert W. Patrick. Chapel Hill, 1965, pp. 249-272.†

6 MEADE, Robert D. "The Relations between Judah P. Benjamin and Jefferson Davis." *J S Hist,* V (1939), 468-478.

7 MOORE, Albert B. *Conscription and Conflict in the Confederacy.* New York, 1924. (The standard monograph.)

8 OATES, Stephen B. "Texas under the Secessionists." *Sw Hist Q,* LXVII (1963), 167-212.

9 OWSLEY, Frank L. *State Rights in the Confederacy.* Chicago, 1925. (The basic study.)

10 PARKS, Joseph H. "State Rights in a Crisis: Governor Joseph E. Brown versus President Jefferson Davis." *J S Hist,* XXXII (1966), 3-24.

11 PATRICK, Rembert W. *Jefferson Davis and His Cabinet.* Baton Rouge, 1944. (The best study of the Confederate government.)

12 PATRICK, Rembert W., ed. *The Opinions of the Confederate Attorneys General, 1861-1865.* Buffalo, 1950.

13 POLLARD, Edward A. *The Lost Cause: A New Southern History of the War of the Confederates.* New York, 1866. (By a critic of Confederate President Davis.)

14 RICHARDSON, James D., ed. *A Compilation of the Messages and Papers of the Confederacy, Including the Diplomatic Correspondence, 1861-1865.* 2 vols. Nashville, 1905.

15 RICHARDSON, Ralph. "The Choice of Jefferson Davis as Confederate President." *J Miss Hist,* XVII (1955), 161-176.

16 RINGOLD, May S. *The Role of the State Legislatures in the Confederacy.* Athens, Ga., 1966.

17 ROBINSON, William M., Jr. *Justice in Grey: A History of the Judicial System of the Confederate States of America.* Cambridge, Mass., 1941.

18 ROBINSON, William M., Jr. "A New Deal in Constitutions." *J S Hist,* IV (1938), 449-461. (Praise for the Confederate Constitution.)

19 ROLAND, Charles P. *The Confederacy.* Chicago, 1960.†

20 ROSS, Fitzgerald. *Cities and Camps of the Confederacy,* ed. Richard B. Harwell, Urbana, 1958.

21 SHOFNER, Jerrell and William W. ROGERS. "Montgomery to Richmond: The Confederacy Selects a Capital." *C W Hist,* X (1964), 155-166.

22 STEPHENSON, Nathaniel W. *The Day of the Confederacy.* New Haven, 1919. (A brief interpretive history.)

23 STUART, Meriwether. "Sanuel Ruth and General R. E. Lee: Disloyalty and the Line of Supply to Fredericksburg, 1862-1863." *Va Mag of Hist & Biog,* LXXI (1963), 35-109.

1 TATUM, Georgia L. *Disloyalty in the Confederacy*. Chapel Hill, 1934. (The standard study.)

2 TREXLER, Harrison A. "The Davis Administration and the Richmond Press, 1861-1865." *J S Hist,* XVI (1950), 177-195.

3 TREXLER, Harrison A. "Jefferson Davis and the Confederate Patronage." *S Atl Q,* XXVIII (1929), 45-58.

4 VANDIVER, Frank E. "The Confederacy and the American Tradition." *J S Hist,* XXVIII (1962), 277-286.

5 VAN RIPER, Paul P. and Harry N. SCHEIBER. "The Confederate Civil Service." *J S Hist,* XXV (1959), 448-470.

6 WILEY, Bell I. and Hirst D. MILHOLLEN. *Embattled Confederates: An Illustrated History of Southerns at War.* New York, 1964.

7 WINTERS, John D. *The Civil War in Louisiana.* Baton Rouge, 1963.

8 WELLMAN, Manly W. *They Took Their Stands: The Founders of the Confederacy*. New York, 1959.

9 WESLEY, C. H. *The Collapse of the Confederacy*. Washington, D.C., 1922.

10 YEARNS, Wilfred B. *The Confederate Congress.* Athens, Ga., 1960. (A basic book.)

See also 7.6, 7.9, 9.9, 11.5, 11.6, 11.7, 11.8, 11.9, 11.10, 11.11, 11.12, 11.13, 11.14, 17.13, 20.3, 26.2, 29.8, 29.9, 30.11, 33.8, 33.9, 33.10, 33.11, 33.12, 33.13, 33.14, 35.4, 35.5, 35.6, 36.2, 36.3, 36.4, 36.9, 38.2.

XII. The Confederacy: Economic, Social, and Intellectual Developments

11 ANDREANO, Ralph L. "A Theory of Confederate Finance." *C W Hist,* II (1956), 21-28.

12 ANDREWS, J. Cutler. "The Confederate Press and Public Morale." *J S Hist,* XXXII (1966), 445-465.

13 ANDREWS, J. Cutler. "The Southern Telegraph Company, 1861-1865: A Chapter in the History of Wartime Communications." *J S Hist,* XXX (1944), 319-344.

14 BLACK, Robert C., III. *The Railroads of the Confederacy*. Chapel Hill, 1952. (A basic book.)

15 CAPPON, Lester J. "Government and Private Industry in the Southern Confederacy," in *Humanistic Studies in Honor of John Calvin Metcalf.* New York, 1941, 151-189.

16 CODDINGTON, Edwin B. "Soldiers' Relief in the Seaboard States of the Confederacy." *Miss Val Hist Rev,* XXXVII (1950), 17-38.

17 DANIEL, W. Harrison. "Bible Publication and Procurement in the Confederacy." *J S Hist,* XXIV (1958), 191-201.

18 DANIEL, W. Harrison. "Southern Protestantism–1861 and After." *C W Hist,* V (1959), 276-282.

19 DEW, Charles B. *Ironmaker to the Confederacy: Joseph R. Anderson and the Tredegar Iron Works.* New Haven, 1966. (A study of the South's most important iron manufactory.)

20 DIAMOND, William. "Imports of the Confederate Government from Europe and Mexico." *J S Hist,* VI (1940), 470-503.

1 HARWELL, Richard B. *Confederate Music.* Chapel Hill, 1950.

2 HARWELL, Richard B. *Songs of the Confederacy.* New York, 1951.

3 HILL, Louise B. *State Socialism in the Confederate States of America.* Charlottesville, 1936.

4 JONES, Katharine M. *Ladies of Richmond.* Indianapolis, 1962.

5 JONES, Katharine M., ed. *Heroines of Dixie: Confederate Women Tell Their Story of the War.* Indianapolis, 1955.

6 LERNER, Eugene M. "Inflation in the Confederacy. 1861-1865," in *Studies in the Quantity Theory of Money,* ed. Milton Friedman. Chicago, 1956, 163-178.

7 LERNER, Eugene M. "Monetary and fiscal Programs of the Confederate Government, 1861-65." *J Pol Econ,* LXII (1954), 506-522.

8 LERNER, Eugene M. "Money, Prices, and Wages in the Confederacy, 1861-65." *J Pol Econ,* LXIII (1955), 20-40.

9 LONN, Ella. *Foreigners in the Confederacy.* Chapel Hill, 1940.

10 LONN, Ella. *Salt as a Factor in the Confederacy.* New York, 1933.

11 MASSEY, Mary E. *Ersatz in the Confederacy.* Columbia, S.C., 1952. (A study of wartime shortages and substitutes in the South.)

12 MASSEY, Mary E. *Refugee Life in the Confederacy.* Baton Rouge, 1964.

13 NICHOLS, James L. "The Tax-in-Kind in the Department of the Trans-Mississippi." *C W Hist,* V (1959), 382-389.

14 PARKS, Joseph H. "A Confederate Trade Center under Federal Occupation: Memphis, 1862 to 1865." *J S Hist,* VII (1941), 289-314.

15 RAMSDELL, Charles W. *Behind the Lines in the Southern Confederacy.* Baton Rouge, 1944. (Brief but important; perhaps the best single work on the Confederate home front.)

16 RAMSDELL, Charles W. "The Confederate Government and the Railroads." *Am Hist Rev,* XXII (1917), 794-810.

17 RAMSDELL, Charles W. "The Control of Manufacturing by the Confederate Government." *Miss Val Hist Rev,* VIII (1921), 231-249.

18 ROLAND, Charles P. *Louisiana Sugar Plantations during the American Civil War.* Leiden, 1957.

19 SCHWAB, John C. *The Confederate States of America, 1861-1865: A Financial and Industrial History of the South during the Civil War.* New York, 1901. (Still the basic book.)

20 SELLERS, James L. "The Economic Incidence of the Civil War in the South." *Miss Val Hist Rev,* XIV (1927), 179-191.

21 SILVER, James W. *Confederate Morale and Church Propaganda.* Tuscaloosa, 1957.

22 SILVER, James W. "Propaganda in the Confederacy." *J S Hist,* XI (1945), 487-503.

23 SIMKINS, Francis B. and James W. PATTON. *The Women of the Confederacy.* Richmond, 1936.

24 TODD, Richard C. *Confederate Finance.* Athens, Ga., 1954. (The best modern treatment.)

25 WILEY, Bell I. *The Plain People of the Confederacy.* Baton Rouge, 1943. (The best study of the impact of the war on southern life.)†

26 WRIGHT, Gordon. "Economic Conditions in the Confederacy as Seen by the French Consuls." *J S Hist,* VII (1941), 195-214.

56 XIII. Slavery and the Negro During the War

1 APTHEKER, Herbert. *The Negro in the Civil War.* New York, 1938.†

2 BANCROFT, Frederic. "The Colonization of American Negroes, 1801-1865," in Jacob E. Cooke, *Frederic Bancroft: Historian.* New York, 1957, 145-263.

3 BECK, Warren A. "Lincoln and Negro Colonization in Central America." *A Lincoln Q,* VI (1950), 162-183.

4 CLEVEN, N. A. N. "Some Plans for Colonizing Liberated Negro Slaves in Hispanic America." *J Neg Hist,* XI (1926), 35-49.

5 CORNISH, Dudley T. *The Sable Arm: Negro Troops in the Union Army, 1861-1865.* New York, 1956. (The standard monograph.)†

6 DUBOIS, W. E. B. "The Negro and the Civil War." *Sci and Soc,* XXV (1961), 347-352.

7 DYER, Brainerd. "The Persistence of the Idea of Negro Colonization." *Pac Hist Rev,* XII (1943), 53-67.

8 DYER, Brainerd. "The Treatment of Colored Union Troops by the Confederates, 1861-1865." *J Neg Hist,* XX (1935), 273-286.

9 FLEMING, Walter L. "Deportation and Colonization: An Attempted Solution of the Race Problem," in *Studies in Southern History . . . Inscribed to William Archibald Dunning.* New York, 1914, 3-30.

10 FRANKLIN, John H., ed. *The Diary of James T. Ayers, Civil War Recruiter.* Springfield, Ill., 1947. (Important account by a man who raised Union regiments among southern Negroes.)

11 FRANKLIN, John H. *The Emancipation Proclamation.* New York, 1963.†

12 HIGGINSON, Thomas W. *Army Life in a Black Regiment.* Boston, 1870.†

13 LOFTON, Williston H. "Northern Labor and the Negro during the Civil War." *J Neg Hist,* XXXIV (1949), 251-273.

14 MC PHERSON, James M. *The Struggle for Equality: Abolitionists and the Negro in the Civil War and Reconstruction.* Princeton, 1964.†

15 MC PHERSON, James M., ed. *The Negro's Civil War: How American Negroes Felt and Acted during the War for the Union.* New York, 1965.

16 QUARLES, Benjamin F. *Lincoln and the Negro.* New York, 1962. (The best book.)

17 SCHEIPS, Paul J. "Lincoln and the Chiriqui Colonization Project." *J Neg Hist,* XXXVII (1952), 418-453.

18 SHANNON, Fred A. "The Federal Government and the Negro Soldier, 1861-1865," *J Neg Hist,* XI (1926), 563-583.

19 STEPHENSON, Nathaniel W. "The Question of Arming the Slaves." *Am Hist Rev,* XVIII (1913), 295-308.

20 SWINT, Henry, ed. *Dear Ones at Home: Letters from Contraband Camps.* Nashville, 1966.

21 THORNBROUGH, Emma L. *Since Emancipation: A Short History of Indiana Negroes, 1863-1963.* Indianapolis, 1963.

22 TREXLER, Harrison A. "The Opposition of Planters to the Employment of Slaves as Laborers by the Confederacy." *Miss Val Hist Rev,* XXVII (1940), 211-224.

1 VOEGELI, V. Jacque. *Free but Not Equal: The Midwest and the Negro during the Civil War.* Chicago, 1967.

2 WAGANDT, Charles L. *The Mighty Revolution: Negro Emancipation in Maryland, 1862-1864.* Baltimore, 1964.

3 WESLEY, Charles H. "The Employment of Negroes as Soldiers in the Confederate Army." *J Neg Hist,* IV (1919), 239-253.

4 WILEY, Bell I. *Southern Negroes, 1861-1865.* New Haven, 1938. (The basic monograph.)†

5 WOOD, Forrest G. *Black Scare: The Racist Response to Emancipation and Reconstruction.* Berkely, 1968.

See also **12**.8, **12**.9, **14**.8, **14**.9, **14**.10, **14**.11, **22**.8, **22**.24, **27**.11, **27**.12.

XIV. Wartime Diplomacy

6 ADAMS, Charles F., Jr. *Seward and the Declaration of Paris: A Forgotten Diplomatic Episode.* Boston, 1912.

7 ADAMS, Charles F., Jr. "The Trent Affair." *Am Hist Rev,* XVII (1912), 540-562.

8 ADAMS, Ephraim D. *Great Britain and the American Civil War.* 2 vols. New York, 1925. (Still the most complete and authoritative treatment.)

9 BAILEY, Thomas A. "The Russian Fleet Myth Re-Examined." *Miss Val Hist Rev,* XXXVIII (1951), 81-90.

10 BAXTER, James P., III. "The British Government and Neutral Rights, 1861-1865." *Am Hist Rev,* XXXIV (1928), 9-29.

11 BAXTER, James P., III, ed. "Papers Relating to Belligerent and Neutral Rights, 1861-1865." *Am Hist Rev,* XXXIV (1928), 77-91.

12 BAXTER, James P., III. "Some British Opinions as to Neutral Rights, 1861 to 1865." *Am J Int Law,* XXIII (1929), 517-537.

13 BELOFF, Max. "Great Britian and the American Civil War." *Hist,* XXXVII (1952), 40-48.

14 BLUMENTHAL, Henry. "Confederate Diplomacy: Popular Notions and International Realities." *J S Hist,* XXXII (1966), 151-171.

15 BLUMENTHAL, Henry. *A Reappraisal of Franco-American Relations, 1830-1871.* Chapel Hill, 1959.

16 BONHAM, Milledge L. *The British Consuls in the Confederacy.* New York, 1911.

17 "Bright-Sumner Letters, 1861-1872." *Proc Mass Hist Soc,* XLIV (1912), 93-164.

18 BULLOCH, James D. *Secret Service of the Confederate States in Europe.* 2 vols. New York, 1884.

19 CASE, Lynn M. *French Opinion on the United States and Mexico, 1860-1867: Extracts from the Reports of the Procureurs Generaux.* New York, 1936.

20 CALLAHAN, James M. *Diplomatic History of the Southern Confederacy.* Baltimore, 1901.

21 CLAUSSEN, Martin P. "Peace Factors in Anglo-American Relations, 1861-1865." *Miss Val Hist Rev,* XXVI (1940), 511-522.

22 COHEN, Victor H. "Charles Sumner and the *Trent* Affair." *J S Hist,* XII (1956), 205-219.

23 COLLYER, C. "Gladstone and the American Civil War." *Proc Leeds Phil Soc,* VI (pt. 8), 583-594.

1 DENNETT, Tyler. "Seward's Far Eastern Diplomacy." *Am Hist Rev,* XXVIII (1922), 45-62.

2 DU BELLET, Paul P. *The Diplomacy of the Confederate Cabinet of Richmond and Its Agents Abroad,* ed. William S. Hoole. Tuscaloosa, 1963.

3 DYER, Brainerd. "Thomas H. Dudley." *C W Hist,* I (1955), 401-413. (Dudley was the influential Union consul at Liverpool.)

4 FERRIS, Nathan L. "The Relations of the United States with South America during the American Civil War." *His-Am Hist Rev,* XXI (1941), 51-78.

5 GINZBERG, Eli. "The Economics of British Neutrality during the American Civil War." *Ag Hist,* X (1936), 147-156.

6 GOLDER, Frank A. "The Russian Fleet and the Civil War." *Am Hist Rev,* XX (1915), 801-812.

7 HARRIS, Thomas L. *The Trent Affair.* Indianapolis, 1896.

8 JONES, Robert H. "The American Civil War in the British Sessional Papers: Catalogue and Commentary." *Proc Am Philos Soc,* CVII (1963), 415-426.

9 JONES, Wilbur D. "The British Conservatives and the American Civil War." *Am Hist Rev,* LVIII (1953), 527-543.

10 JONES, Wilbur D. *Confederate Rams at Birkenhead.* Tuscaloosa, 1961.

11 JORDAN, Donaldson and Edwin J. PRATT. *Europe and the American Civil War.* Boston, 1931. (Largely a study of public opinion.)

12 McDIARMID, Alice M. "American Civil War Precedents: Their Nature, Application, and Extension." *Am Int Law,* XXXIV (1940), 220-237.

13 MacDONALD, Helen G. *Canadian Public Opinion on the American Civil War.* New York, 1926.

14 MAYNARD, Douglas H. "The Forbes-Aspinwall Mission." *Miss Val Hist Rev,* XLV (1958), 67-89.

15 MAYNARD, Douglas H. "Plotting the Escape of the *Alabama,*" *J S Hist,* XX (1954), 197-209.

16 MAYNARD, Douglas H. "Union Efforts to Prevent the Escape of the 'Alabama'." *Miss Val Hist Rev,* XLI (1954), 41-60.

17 NAGENGAST, William E. "The Visit of the Russian Fleet to the United States: Were Americans Deceived?" *Russian Rev,* VIII (1949), 46-55.

18 NEWTON, A. P. "Anglo-American Relations during the Civil War, 1860-1865," in A. W. Ward and G. P. Gooch, eds., *The Cambridge History of British Foreign Policy.* Cambridge, Eng., 1923, II, 488-521.

19 OATES, Stephen B. "Henry Hotze: Confederate Agent Abroad." *Historian,* XXVII (1965), 131-154.

20 OWSLEY, Frank L. "America and the Freedom of the Seas, 1861-1865," in Avery O. Craven, ed., *Essays in Honor of William E. Dodd.* Chicago, 1935, 194-256.

21 OWSLEY, Frank L. and Harriet C. OWSLEY. *King Cotton Diplomacy: Foreign Relations of the Confederate States of America.* 2nd ed. Chicago, 1959. (The definitive treatment.)

22 PERKINS, Dexter. *The Monroe Doctrine, 1826-1867.* Baltimore, 1933.

23 PIERCE, Edward L., ed. "Letters of Richard Cobden to Charles Sumner, 1860-1865." *Am Hist Rev,* II (1897), 306-319.

24 POLE, J. R. *Abraham Lincoln and the Working Classes of Britain.* London, 1959.†

1 POMEROY, Earl S. "The Myth After the Russian Fleet, 1863." *N Y Hist,* XXXI (1950), 169-176.

2 SCHMIDT, Louis B. "The Influence of Wheat and Cotton on Anglo-American Relations during the Civil War." *Iowa J Hist and Pol,* XVI (1918), 400-439.

3 SEARS, Louis M. "A Confederate Diplomat at the Court of Napoleon III." *Am Hist Rev,* XXVI (1921), 255-281.

4 STERN, Philip Van Doren. *When the Guns Roared: World Aspects of the American Civil War.* Garden City, N.Y., 1965.

5 THOMAS, Benjamin P. *Russo-American Relations, 1815-1867.* Baltimore, 1930.

6 TRESCOT, Edward A., ed. "The Confederacy and the Declaration of Paris." *Am Hist Rev,* XXIII (1918), 826-835.

7 TYRNER-TYRNAUER, A. R. *Lincoln and the Emperors.* New York, 1962. (Deals especially with Austrian and Belgian reactions to the war.)

8 WEST, W. Reed. *Contemporary French Opinion on the American Civil War.* Baltimore, 1924.

9 WINKS, Robin. *Canada and the United States: The Civil War Years.* Baltimore, 1960.

See also **5**.10, **5**.11, **5**.12, **5**.13, **5**.14, **6**.10, **9**.8, **13**.1, **13**.2, **13**.3, **20**.8, **22**.17, **23**.19, **25**.5, **25**.6, **26**.4, **27**.3, **27**.4, **31**.4, **31**.5, **31**.6, **31**.7, **31**.8, **32**.9, **32**.10.

XV. Historiography of Reconstruction

10 BEALE, Howard K. "On Rewriting Reconstruction History." *Am Hist Rev,* XLV (1940), 807-827.

11 CASTEL, Albert. "Andrew Johnson: His Historiographical Rise and Fall." *Mid-Am,* XLV (1963), 175-184.

12 FRANKLIN, John Hope. "Whither Reconstruction Historiography?" *J Neg Ed,* XVII (1948), 446-461.

13 GALLAWAY, B. P. "Economic Determinism in Reconstruction Historiography." *Sw Soc Sci Q,* XLVI (1965), 244-254.

14 GREEN, Fletcher M. "Introduction." *The Civil War and Reconstruction in Florida,* by William W. Davis (Gainesville, Fla., 1964), xiii-xlv.

15 HARPER, Alan D. "William A. Dunning: The Historian as Nemesis." *C W Hist,* X (1964), 54-66.

16 KRUG, Mark M. "On Rewriting the Story of Reconstruction in the U.S. History Textbooks." *J Neg Hist,* XLVI (1961), 133-153.

17 LYND, Staughton. "Rethinking Slavery and Reconstruction." *J Neg Hist,* L (1965), 198-209.

18 SIMKINS, Francis B. "New Viewpoints of Southern Reconstruction." *J S Hist,* V (1939), 49-61.

19 TAYLOR, Alrutheus A. "Historians of Reconstruction." *J Neg Hist,* XXIII (1938), 16-34.

20 WEISBERGER, Bernard A. "The Dark and Bloody Ground of Reconstruction Historiography." *J S Hist,* XXV (1959), 427-447.

21 WESLEY, Charles H. " W. E. B. DuBois–the Historian." *J Neg Hist,* L (1965), 147-162.

22 WHARTON, Vernon L. "Reconstruction," in *Writing Southern History,* ed. Arthur S. Link and Rembert W. Patrick. Chapel Hill, 1965, pp. 295-315.†

23 WILLIAMS, T. Harry. "An Analysis of Some Reconstruction Attitudes." *J S Hist,* XII (1946), 469-486.

XVI. General Histories of Reconstruction

1 ALLEN, James S. *Reconstruction: The Battle for Democracy.* New York, 1937. (A Marxist interpretation.)†

2 BOWERS, Claude G. *The Tragic Era: The Revolution after Lincoln.* Boston, 1929. (Popular history, luridly anti-Negro.)†

3 BUCK, Paul H. *The Road to Reunion, 1865-1900.* Boston, 1937. (The standard study of sectional reconciliation.)†

4 BURGER, Nash K. and John K. BETTERSWORTH. *South of Appomattox.* New York, 1959.

5 CARTER, Hodding. *The Angry Scar: the Story of Reconstruction.* New York, 1959.

6 COULTER, E. Merton. *The South during Reconstruction, 1865-1877.* Baton Rouge, 1947.

7 DU BOIS, W. E. Burghardt. *Black Reconstruction, 1860-1880.* New York, 1935. (A quasi-Marxist treatment, emphasizing the achievements of Negroes.)†

8 DU BOIS, W. E. Berghardt. "Reconstruction and Its Benefits." *Am Hist Rev,* XV (1910), 781-799.

9 DUNNING, William A. *Reconstruction, Political and Economic, 1865-1877.* New York, 1907.†

10 FLEMING, Walter Lynwood. *The Sequel of Appomattox: A Chronicle of the Reunion of the States.* New Haven, 1919.

11 FLEMING, Walter Lynwood, ed. *Documentary History of Reconstruction: Political, Military, Social, Religious, Educational and Industrial, 1865 to the Present Time.* 2 vols. Cleveland, 1906. (The basic documentary collection.)†

12 FRANKLIN, John Hope. *Reconstruction after the Civil War.* Chicago, 1961.†

13 HENRY, Robert Selph. *The Story of Reconstruction.* Indianapolis, 1938.

14 HYMAN, Harold M., ed. *New Frontiers of the American Reconstruction.* Urbana, 1966.

15 JOSEPHSON, Matthew. *The Politicos, 1865-1896.* New York, 1938. (A spirited, cynical account of national politics.)†

16 MC PHERSON, Edward, ed. *The Political History of the United States. . . during. . .Reconstruction.* 2d ed. Washington, D.C., 1875. (A useful compilation of political documents.)

17 NEVINS, Allan. *The Emergence of Modern America, 1865-1878.* New York, 1928. (A history of social and economic developments.)

18 OBERHOLTZER, Ellis P. *A History of the United States since the Civil War.* 5 vols. New York, 1917-1937. (The most comprehensive general history of the period.)

19 PATRICK, Rembert W. *The Reconstruction of the Nation.* New York, 1967.†

20 SEFTON, James E. *The United States Army and Reconstruction, 1865-1867.* Baton Rouge, 1967.

1 SHENTON, James P., ed. *The Reconstruction: A Documentary History of the South after the War, 1865-1877.* New York, 1963.†

2 STAMPP, Kenneth M. *The Era of Reconstruction, 1865-1877.* New York, 1965. (The best modern treatment.)†

3 TRELEASE, Allen W. "Who Were the Scalawags?" *J S Hist,* XXIX (1963), 445-468. (See also rebuttal by David Donald, *ibid.,* XXX (1964), 253-257.)

4 WHITE, Leonard D. *The Republican Era, 1869-1901: A Study in Administrative History.* New York, 1958.†

XVII. Presidential Reconstruction

5 BEALE, Howard K. *The Critical Year: A Study of Andrew Johnson and Reconstruction.* 2d ed. New York, 1958. (A strongly pro-Johnson work, emphasizing the economic motivation of his opponents.)

6 BROCK, William R. *An American Crisis: Congress and Reconstruction, 1865-1867.* New York, 1963. (A work critical of Johnson and favorable to the Radical Republicans.)†

7 CHADSEY, Charles E. *The Struggle between President Johnson and Congress over Reconstruction.* New York, 1896.

8 CLARK, John G. "Radicals and Moderates on the Joint Committee on Reconstruction." *Mid-Am,* XLV (1963), 175-184.

9 CLEMENCEAU, Georges. *American Reconstruction, 1865-1870, and the Impeachment of President Johnson,* trans, and ed. Fernand Baldensperger. New York, 1928. (Contemporary observations by the future French premier.)

10 COX, LaWanda and John H. COX. *Politics, Principle, and Prejudice, 1865-1866.* New York, 1963. (A strongly anti-Johnson work, stressing the Negrophobic views of his supporters.)

11 DEWITT, David M. *The Impeachment and Trial of Andrew Johnson.* New York, 1903.

12 DONALD, David. *The Politics of Reconstruction, 1863-1867.* Baton Rouge, 1965. (An application of the quantitative techniques to the study of congressional behavior.)

13 DORRIS, Jonathan T. *Pardon and Amnesty under Lincoln and Johnson.* Chapel Hill, 1953.

14 DUNNING, William A. "More Light on Andrew Johnson," in Dunning's *Truth in History.* New York, 1937, pp.80-107.

15 GIPSON, Lawrence H. "The Statesmanship of President Johnson: A Study of the Presidential Reconstruction Policy." *Miss Val Hist Rev,* II (1915), 363-383.

16 HESSELTINE, William B. *Lincoln's Plan of Reconstruction.* Tuscaloosa, 1960.

1 HYMAN, Harold M. "Johnson, Stanton, and Grant: A Reconsideration of the Army's Role in the Events Leading to Impeachment." *Am Hist Rev,* LXVI (1960), 85-100.

2 MC CARTHY, Charles H. *Lincoln's Plan of Reconstruction.* New York, 1901.

3 RUSS, William A., Jr. "The Struggle between President Lincoln and Congress over Disfranchisement of Rebels." *Susquehanna Univ Stud,* III (1947), 177-205, and III (1948), 221-243.

4 SCOTT, Eben G. *Reconstruction during the Civil War in the U.S.A.* Boston, 1895.

See also **7**.1, **8**.5, **8**.7, **8**.8, **9**.10, **9**.11, **13**.6, **13**.7, **19**.7, **19**.9, **19**.10, **19**.11, **19**.12, **19**.13, **19**.14, **19**.15, **20**.4, **20**.5, **20**.6, **23**.1, **25**.2, **26**.5, **26**.9, **29**.6, **29**.7, **33**.4, **33**.5, **33**.6, **33**.7, **33**.15, **33**.16, **33**.17, **34**.1, **34**.2, **34**.6, **34**.8, **35**.9, **35**.10, **36**.6, **36**.7, **37**.6, **37**.7, **37**.8.

XVIII. The Radicals in Power

5 COLEMAN, Charles H. *The election of 1868: The Democratic Effort to Regain Control.* New York, 1933.

6 DEARING, Mary R. *Veterans in Politics: The Story of the G.A.R.* Baton Rouge, 1952.

7 DUNNING, William A. "The Second Birth of the Republican Party." *Am Hist Rev,* XVI (1910), 56-63.

8 HOUSE, Albert V., Jr. "Northern Congressional Democrats as Defenders of the South during Reconstruction." *J S Hist,* VI (1940), 46-71.

9 HYMAN, Harold M., ed. *The Radical Republicans and Reconstruction, 1861-1870.* Indianapolis, 1967. (A valuable compilation of contemporary writings.)†

10 KENDRICK, Benjamin B. *The Journal of the Joint Committee of Fifteen on Reconstruction, 39th Congress, 1865-1867.* New York, 1914.

11 LERCHE, Charles O., Jr. "Congressional Interpretations of the Guarantee of a Republican Form of Government during Reconstruction." *J S Hist,* XV (1949), 192-211.

12 LINDEN, Glenn M. "'Radicals' and Economic Policies: The House of Representatives, 1861-1873." *C W Hist,* XIII (1967), 51-65.

13 MC PHERSON, James M. "Abolitionists, Woman Suffrage and the Negro, 1865-1869." *Mid-Am,* XLVII (1965), 40-47.

14 MONTGOMERY, David. *Beyond Equality: Labor and the Radical Republicans, 1862-1872.* New York, 1967.

15 MORROW, Ralph E. *Northern Methodism and Reconstruction,* East Lansing, Mich., 1956.

16 NOYES, Edward, "The Ohio G.A.R. and Politics from 1866-1900." *Ohio Arch and Hist Q,* LV (1946), 79-105.

17 PERZEL, Edward S. "Alexander Long, Salmon P. Chase and the Election of 1868." *Cincinnati Hist Soc Bull,* XXIII (1965), 3-18.

18 PRIMM, James N. "The G.A.R. in Missouri, 1866-1870." *J S Hist,* XX (1954), 356-375.

19 RUSS, William A., Jr. "The Influence of the Methodist Press upon Radical Reconstruction (1865-1868)." *Susquehanna Univ Stud,* I (1937), 51-62.

20 RUSS, William A., Jr. "Registration and Disfranchisement under Radical Reconstruction." *Miss Val Hist Rev,* XXI (1934), 163-180.

1 RUSS, William A., Jr. "Was There Danger of a Second Civil War during Reconstruction?" *Miss Val Hist Rev,* XXV (1938), 39-58.

2 SCROGGS, Jack B. "Carpetbagger Constitutional Reform in the South Atlantic States, 1867-1868." *J S Hist,* XXVII (1961), 475-493.

3 SCROGGS, Jack B. "Southern Reconstruction: A Radical View." *J S Hist,* XXIV (1958), 407-439.

4 SHORTREED, Margaret. "The Anti-Slavery Radicals, 1840-1868." *Past and Present,* XVI (1959), 65-87.

5 WILLIAMS, Helen J. and Harry WILLIAMS. "Wisconsin Republicans and Reconstruction, 1865-70." *Wisc Mag Hist,* XXIII (1939), 17-39.

6 WOODWARD, C Vann. "The Seeds of Failure in Radical Race Policy." *Proc Am Philos Soc,* CX (1966), 1-9.

See also **8**.14, **9**.4, **9**.6, **9**.10, **9**.11, **9**.12, **9**.13, **12**.3, **12**.8, **12**.9, **13**.1, **13**.2, **13**.3, **13**.6, **13**.7, **14**.4, **14**.5, **14**.6, **14**.13, **16**.1, **19**.14, **20**.4, **20**.5, **20**.6, **26**.5, **26**.9, **27**.7, **31**.12, **31**.13, **31**.14, **33**.1, **33**.2, **33**.3, **33**.4, **33**.5, **33**.6, **33**.7, **33**.15, **33**.16, **33**.17, **34**.1, **34**.2, **34**.6, **34**.7, **34**.8, **35**.9, **35**.10, **36**.6, **36**.7.

XIX. The Nation After the War: Economic and Social Problems

7 ABELL, Aaron I. *The Urban Impact on American Protestantism, 1865-1900.* Cambridge, Mass., 1943.

8 ADAMS, Charles Francis, Jr. and Henry ADAMS. *Chapters of Erie, and Other Essays.* Boston, 1871. (Astute, cynical commentary on postwar economic manipulation.)

9 ANDERSON, George L. "The Proposed Resumption of Silver Payments in 1873." *Pac Hist Rev,* VIII (1939), 301-316.

10 ANDERSON, George L. "Western Attitudes toward National Banks, 1873-74." *Miss Val Hist Rev,* XXIII (1936), 205-216.

11 BARNETT, Paul. "The Crime of 1873 Reexamined." *Ag Hist,* XXXVIII (1964), 178-181.

12 BARRETT, Don C. *The Greenbacks and Resumption of Specie Payments.* Cambridge, Mass., 1931.

13 BEALE, Howard K. "The Tariff and Reconstruction." *Am Hist Rev,* XXXV (1930), 276-294.

14 BENSON, Lee. *Merchants, Farmers, and Railroads: Railroad Regulation and New York Politics, 1850-1887.* Cambridge, Mass., 1955.

15 BROEHL, Wayne G., Jr. *The Molly Maguires.* Cambridge, Mass., 1964.

16 BUCK, Solon J. *The Granger Movement.* Cambridge, Mass., 1913.†

17 COBEN, Stanley. "Northeastern Business and Radical Reconstruction: A Re-examination." *Miss Val Hist Rev,* XLVI (1959), 67-90. (Challenges the stereotype of monolithic "big business" backing the Radical policies.)

18 COCHRAN, Thomas C., and William MILLER. *The Age of Enterprise.* New York, 1942. (A brilliantly executed social history of American business.)†

19 COCHRAN, Thomas C. "The Legend of the Robber Barons." *Penn Mag Hist and Biog,* LXXIV (1950), 307-321.

20 DESTLER, Chester M. *American Radicalism, 1865-1901: Essays and Documents.* New London, 1946. (Contains important articles on monetary reforms proposed after the war.)†

1 DESTLER, Chester M. "The Opposition of American Businessmen to Social Control during the 'Gilded Age'." *Miss Val Hist Rev,* XXXIX (1953), 641-672.

2 FELS, Rendigs. *American Business Cycles, 1865-1897.* Chapel Hill, 1959.

3 FINE, Sidney. *Laissez Faire and the General Welfare State: A Study of Conflict in American Thought, 1865-1901.* Ann Arbor, 1956.†

4 FITE, Gilbert C. *The Farmer's Frontier, 1865-1900.* New York, 1966.

5 FRIEDMAN, Milton, and Anna J. SCHWARTZ. *A Monetary History of the United States, 1867-1960.* Princeton, 1963.

6 GRAHAM, Frank D. "International Trade under Depreciated Paper: The United States, 1862-79." *Q J Econ,* XXXVI (1922), 220-273.

7 GRISWOLD, Wesley S. *A Work of Giants: Building the First Transcontinental Railroad.* New York, 1962.

8 GRODINSKY, Julius. *The Iowa Pool: A Study in Railroad Competition, 1870-1884.* Chicago, 1950.

9 HENRY, Robert S. "The Railroad Land Grant Legend in American History Texts." *Miss Val Hist Rev,* XXXII(1945), 171-194. (See also the replies evoked by this essay, *ibid.,* 557-576.)

10 JOSEPHSON, Matthew. *1861-1901.* New York, 1934. (A spirited, muckraking attack upon the captains of American business.)†

11 KIRKLAND, Edward C. *Dream and Thought in the Business Community, 1860-1900.* Ithaca. 1956.†

12 KIRKLAND, Edward C. *Industry Comes of Age: Business, Labor, and Public Policy.* New York, 1961. (The best general survey.)

13 KIRKLAND, Edward C. "The Robber Barons Revisited." *Am Hist Rev,* LXVI (1960), 68-73.

14 MC CAGUE, James. *Moguls and Iron Men: The Story of the First Transcontinental Railroad.* New York, 1964.

15 MC CARTNEY, Ernest R. *Crisis of 1873.* Minneapolis, 1935.

16 MC KELVEY, Blake. *The Urbanization of America, 1860-1915.* New Brunswick, N.J., 1963.

17 MERK, Frederick. "Eastern Antecedents of the Grangers." *Ag Hist,* XXIII (1949), 1-8.

18 MILLER, George H. "Origins of the Iowa Granger Law." *Miss Val Hist Rev,* XL (1954), 657-680.

19 MITCHELL, Wesley C. *Gold, Prices, and Wages under the Greenback Standard.* Berkeley, 1908.

20 NUGENT, Walter T. K. *The Money Question during Reconstruction.* New York, 1967.

21 PATTERSON, Robert T. *Federal Debt-Management Policies, 1867-1879.* Durham, N.C., 1954.

22 REZNECK, Samuel. "Distress, Relief and Discontent during the Depression of 1873-78." *J Pol Econ,* LVIII (1950), 494-512.

23 RIEGEL, Robert E. *The Story of the Western Railroads.* New York, 1926.

1 ROTHSTEIN, Morton. "America in the International Rivalry for the British Wheat Market, 1860-1914." *Miss Val Hist Rev,* XLVII (1960), 401-418.

2 SHANNON, Fred A. *The Farmer's Last Frontier: Agriculture, 1860-1897.* New York, 1945. (An admirable survey.)

3 SHARKEY, Robert P. *Money, Class, and Party: An Economic Study in Civil War and Reconstruction.* Baltimore, 1959.†

4 SHIPLEY, Max L. "The Background and Legal Aspects of the Pendleton Plan." *Miss Val Hist Rev,* XXIV (1937), 329-340.

5 SIGMUND, Elwin W. "The Granger Cases: 1877 or 1876?" *Am Hist Rev,* LVIII (1953), 571-574.

6 TIMBERLAKE, Richard H., Jr.. "Ideological Factors in Specie Resumption and Treasury Policy." *J Econ Hist,* XXIV (1964), 29-52.

7 UNGER, Irwin F. *The Greenback Era: A Social and Political History of American Finance, 1865-1879.* Princeton, 1964. (The definitive study, combing sound economic analysis and fine historical insight.)

8 WEINSTEIN, Allen. "Was There a 'Crime of 1873'? The Case of the Demonetized Dollar." *J Am Hist,* LIV (1967), 307-326.

9 WELLS, O.V. "The Depression of 1873-79." *Ag Hist,* XI (1937), 237-249.

10 WINTHER, Oscar O. *The Transportation Frontier: Trans-Mississippi West, 1865-1890.* New York, 1964.

11 WOOLFOLK, George R. *The Cotton Regency: The Northern Merchants and Reconstruction, 1865-1880.* New York, 1959.

See also **12**.2, **15**.4, **29**.11, **32**.8.

XX. The South During Reconstruction: State and Local Studies

Alabama

12 ALEXANDER, Thomas B. "Persistent Whiggery in Alabama and the Lower South, 1860-1867." *Ala Rev,* XII (1959), 35-52.

13 BOND, Horace Mann. "Social and Economic Forces in Alabama Reconstruction." *J Neg Hist,* XXIII (1938), 290-348.

14 DUBOSE, John Witherspoon. *Alabama's Tragic Decade: Ten Years of Alabama, 1865-1874.* Birmingham, 1940.

15 FLEMING, Walter Lynwood. *Civil War and Reconstruction in Alabama.* New York, 1905. (Still the basic monograph, through marred by an anti-Negro bias.)

16 WOOLFOLK, Sarah Van. "Carpetbaggers in Alabama: Tradition versus Truth." *Ala Rev,* XV (1962), 133-144.

Arkansas

1 CLAYTON, Powell. *The Aftermath of the Civil War in Arkansas.* New York, 1915.

2 HARRELL, J. M. *The Brooks and Baxter War: A History of the Reconstruction Period in Arkansas.* St. Louis, 1893.

3 STAPLES, Thomas S. *Reconstruction in Arkansas, 1862-1874.* New York, 1923. (The standard monograph.)

4 THOMAS, David Y. *Arkansas in War and Reconstruction, 1861-1874.* Little Rock, 1926.

Florida

5 DAVIS, William W. *The Civil war and Reconstruction in Florida.* New York, 1913. (The standard monograph.)

6 SHOFNER, Jerrell H. "Political Reconstruction in Florida." *Fla Hist Q,* XLI (1963), 356-374.

7 SHOFNER, Jerrell H. "Political Reconstruction in Florida." *Fla Hist Q,* XLV (1966), 145-170.

8 SMITH, George Winston. "Carpetbag Imperialism in Florida, 1862-1868." *Fla Hist Q,* XXVII (1948), 99-130; and XXVII (1949), 260-299.

Georgia

9 CONWAY, Alan. *The Reconstruction of Georgia.* Minneapolis, 1966. (A revisionist work, friendly to the Radical program.)

10 COULTER, E. Merton. "Henry M. Turner: Georgia Negro Preacher–Politician during the Reconstruction Era." *Ga Hist Q,* XLVIII (1964), 371-410.

11 GOTTLIEB, Manuel. "The Land Question in Georgia during Reconstruction." *Sci and Soc,* III (1939), 356-388. (A Marxist view.)

12 SHADGETT, Olive H. *The Republican Party in Georgia from Reconstruction through 1900.* Athens, Ga., 1964.

13 THOMPSON, Clara M. *Reconstruction in Georgia, Economic, Social, Political, 1865-1872.* New York, 1915. (The standard monograph.)

14 WOOLEY, Edwin C. *The Reconstruction of Georgia.* New York, 1901.

Kentucky

15 COULTER, E. Merton. *The Civil War and Readjustment in Kentucky.* Chapel Hill, 1926. (The standard monograph.)

Louisiana

1 CASKEY, Willie M. *Secession and Restoration of Louisiana.* University, La., 1938

2 FICKLEN, John R. *History of Reconstruction in Louisiana (through 1868).* Baltimore, 1910. (Along with Miss Lonn's book, the standard treatment.)

3 HARLAN, Louis R. "Desegregation in New Orleans Public Schools during Reconstruction." *Am Hist Rev,* LXVII (1962), 663-675.

4 LONN, Ella. *Reconstruction in Louisiana after 1868.* New York, 1918.

5 MC GINTY, Garnie W. *Louisiana Redeemed: The Overthrow of the Carpet-Bag Rule, 1876-1880.* New Orleans, 1941.

6 REYNOLDS, Donald E. "The New Orleans Riot of 1866, Reconsidered." *La Hist,* V (1964), 5-28.

7 SHUGG, Roger W. *Origins of Class Struggle in Louisiana: A Social History of White Farmers and Laborers during Slavery and After, 1840-1876.* University, La., 1939.

8 WILLIAMS, T. Harry. "The Louisiana Unification Movement of 1873." *J S Hist,* XI (1945), 349-369. (A seminal revisionist essay.)

See also **28**.3, **36**.10.

Maryland

9 MYERS, W. S. *The Self-Reconstruction of Maryland, 1864-1867.* Baltimore, 1909.

Mississippi

10 AMES, Blanche Butler, comp. *Chronicles from the Nineteenth Century: Family Letters of Blanche Butler and Albert Ames.* 2 vols. Clinton, Mass., 1957. Revealing letters of the carpetbag Governor and Senator.)

11 APTHEKER, Herbert. "Mississippi Reconstruction and the Negro Leader Charles Caldwell." *Sci and Soc,* XI (1947), 340-371. A Marxist view.)

12 DONALD, David. "The Scalawag in Mississippi Reconstruction." *J S Hist,* X (1944), 447-460. (Stresses the role played by former Whigs in the Republican party.).

13 GARNER, James W. *Reconstruction in Mississippi.* New York, 1901. (The standard monograph.)

14 HARRIS, William C. *Presidential Reconstruction in Mississippi.* Baton Rouge, 1967.

15 LEFTWICH, George J. "Reconstruction in Monroe County." *Pub Miss Hist Soc,* IX (1906), 53-84. (One of many such detailed local studies published in this series.)

1 MC NEILLY, J. S. "The Enforcement Act of 1871 and the Ku Klux Klan in Mississippi." *Pub Miss Hist Soc,* IX (1906), 109-171.

2 PEREYRA, Lillian A. *James Lusk Alcorn, Persistent Whig.* Baton Rouge, 1966. (Biography of the scalawag Governor and Senator.)

See also **20**.8.

Missouri

3 PARRISH, William E. *Missouri under Radical Rule.* Columbia, Mo., 1965.

4 PETERSON, Norma L. *Freedom and Franchise: The Political Career of B. Gratz Brown.* Columbia, Mo., 1965.

North Carolina

5 EVANS, W. Mckee. *Ballots and Fence Rails: Reconstruction on the Lower Cape Fear.* Chapel Hill, 1966.

6 HAMILTON, J. G. de Roulhac. *Reconstruction in North Carolina.* New York, 1914, (The standard monograph.)

See also **24**.1, **35**.7, **35**.8, **38**.1.

South Carolina

7 DURDEN, Robert F. "The Prostrate State Revisited: James S. Pike and South Carolina Reconstruction." *J Neg Hist.* XXXIX (1954), 87-110.

8 MACAULAY, Neill W. "South Carolina Reconstruction Historiography." *S C Hist Mag,* LXV (1964), 20-32.

9 PIKE, James S. *The Prostrate State: South Carolina under Negro Government.* New York, 1874.† (An influential work by a contemporary Northern newspaperman, who was strongly anti-Negro.)

10 REYNOLDS, John S. *Reconstruction in South Carolina, 1865-1877.* Columbia, S.C., 1905. (A political narrative, with a Bourbon viewpoint.)

11 ROSE, Willie Lee. *Rehearsal for Reconstruction: The Port Royal Experiment. Indianapolis, 1964.†*

12 SHEPPARD, William A. *Red Shirts Remembered: Southern Brigadiers of the Reconstruction Period.* Spartanburg, S.C., 1940.

13 SIMKINS, Francis B. and Robert H. WOODY. *South Carolina during Reconstruction.* Chapel Hill, 1932. (A basic revisionist monograph.)

See also **27**.10, **28**.2.

Tennessee

14 ALEXANDER, Thomas B. *Political Reconstruction in Tennessee.* Nashville, 1950. (A revisionist study of great significance.)

15 ALEXANDER, Thomas B. "Whiggery and Reconstruction in Tennessee." *J S Hist,* XVI (1950), 291-305.

1 FERTIG, James W. *The Secession and Reconstruction of Tennessee.* Chicago, 1898.

2 HOLMES, Jack D. L. "The Underlying Causes of the Memphis Race Riot of 1866." *Tenn Hist Q,* XVII (1958), 195-221.

3 PATTON, James W. *Unionism and Reconstruction in Tennessee, 1860-1869.* Chapel Hill, 1934. (The standard monograph.)

4 QUEENER, Verton M. "A Decade of East Tennessee Republicanism, 1867-1876." *E Tenn Hist Soc Pub,* No. 14 (1942), 59-85.

5 QUEENER, Verton M. "The East Tennessee Republican as a Minority Party, 1870-1896." *E Tenn Hist Soc Pub,* No. 15 (1943), 49-73.

6 QUEENER, Verton M. "The Origin of the Republican Party in East Tennessee." *E Tenn Hist Soc Pub,* No. 13 (1941), 66-90.

See also **7**.9.

Texas

7 CASDORPH, Paul C. *A History of the Republican Party in Texas, 1865-1965.* Austin, Tex., 1965.

8 NUNN, W. C. *Texas under the Carpetbaggers.* Austin, Tex., 1962.

9 RAMSDELL, Charles W. *Reconstruction in Texas.* New York, 1910. (The basic monograph.)

Virginia

10 ECKENRODE, H. J. *The Political History of Virginia during the Reconstruction.* Baltimore, 1904. (The only comprehensive, if thoroughly inadequate, account.)

11 JONES, Wilbur D., ed. "A British Report on Postwar Virginia." *Va Mag Hist & Biog,* LXIX (1961), 346-352. (Observations of Sir Frederick Bruce.)

See also **25**.3.

XXI. The South After the War: Economic, Social, and Intellectual Developments

12 BERTHOFF, Rowland T. "Southern Attitudes toward Immigration." *J S Hist* XVII (1951), 328-360.

13 CLARK, Thomas D. "The Furnishing and Supply System in Southern Agriculture since 1865." *J S Hist,* X11 (1946), 24-44.

14 CLARK, Thomas D. "The Post-Civil War Economy in the South." *Am Jew Hist Soc Q,* LV (1966), 424-433.

15 DOSTER, James F. "Were the Southern Railroads Destroyed by War?" *C W Hist,* VII (1961), 310-320.

1 GATES, Paul W. "Federal Land Policy in the South, 1866-1888." *J S Hist,* VI (1940), 303-330.

2 GOODRICH, Carter. "Public Aid to Railroads in the Reconstruction South." *Pol Sci Q,* LXXI (1956), 407-442.

3 GRIFFIN, Richard W. "Problems of the Southern Cotton Planters after the Civil War." *Ga Hist Q,* XXXIX (1955), 103-117.

4 HALL, Wade. *The Smiling Phoenix: Southern Humor from 1865 to 1914.* Gainesville, 1965.

5 HIGHSMITH, William E. "Some Aspects of Reconstruction in the Heart of Louisiana." *J S Hist,* XIII (1947), 460-491. (Important study of land tenure.)

6 KNIGHT, Edgar W. *The Influence of Reconstruction on Education in the South.* New York, 1913.

7 LERNER, Eugene M. "Southern Output and Agricultural Income, 1860-1880." *Ag Hist,* XXXIII (1959), 117-125.

8 MITCHELL, Broadus and George S. MITCHELL. *The Industrial Revolution in the South.* Baltimore, 1930.

9 SALOUTOS, Theodore. "Southern Agriculture and the Problems of Readjustment, 1865-1877." *Ag Hist,* XXX (1956), 58-76.

10 SHUGG, Roger W. "Survival of the Plantation System in Louisiana."*J S Hist,* III (1937), 311-325. (Challenges the stereotype that the war broke up southern plantations.)

11 STOVER, John F. *The Railroads of the South, 1865-1900.* Chapel Hill, 1955. (The standard account.)

12 SWINT, Henry L. *The Northern Teacher in the South, 1862-1870.* Nashville, 1941.

13 TILLEY, Nannie M. *The Bright Tobacco Industry, 1860-1929.* Chapel Hill, 1948.

14 WILEY, Bell I. "Vicissitudes of Early Reconstruction Farming in the Lower Mississippi Valley." *J S Hist,* III (1937), 441-452.

15 WOODMAN, Harold D. "The Decline of Cotton Factorage after the Civil War." *Am Hist Rev,* LXXI (1966), 1219-1236.

16 ZEICHNER, Oscar. "The Transition from Slave to Free Agricultural Labor in the Southern States." *Ag Hist,* XIII (1939), 22-32.

XXII. The Negro, the Freedmen's Bureau, and the Ku Klux Klan

17 ABBOTT, Martin "Free Land, Free Labor, and the Freedmen's Bureau." *Ag Hist,* XXX (1956), 150-157.

18 ABBOTT, Martin. *The Freedmen's Bureau in South Carolina, 1865-1872.* Chapel Hill, 1967.

19 BENTLEY, George R. *A History of the Freedmen's Bureau.* Philadelphia, 1955. (The standard account.)

1 BOND, Horace M. *Negro Education in Alabama: A Study in Cotton and Steel.* Washington, D.C., 1939. (A basic revisionist work.)

2 BOYD, Willis D. "Negro Colonization in the Reconstruction Era, 1865-1870." *Ga Hist Q,* XL (1956), 360-382.

3 BULLOCK, Henry A. *A History of Negro Education in the South from 1609 to the Present.* Cambridge, Mass., 1967.

4 COX, John and La Wanda COX. "General O. O. Howard and the 'Misrepresented Bureau'" *J S Hist,* XIX (1953), 427-456.

5 COX, LaWanda. "The Promise of Land for the Freedmen." *Miss Val Hist Rev,* XLV (1958), 413-440.

6 DONALD, Henderson H. *The Negro Freedman:. . . The American Negro in the Early Years after Emancipation.* New York, 1952. (The only comprehensive study, but anti-Negro in tone.)

7 DYSON, Walter. *Howard University, the Capstone of Negro Education.* Washington, D.C., 1941.

8 FISHEL, Leslie H. "The Negro in Northern Politics, 1870-1900." *Miss Val Hist Rev,* XLII (1955), 466-489.

9 FLEMING, Walter L. *The Freedmen's Savings Bank.* Chapel Hill, 1927.

10 HORN, Stanley F. *Invisible Empire: The Story of the Ku Klux Klan, 1866-1871.* Boston, 1939. (The best general narrative.)

11 KESSLER, Sidney H. "The Organization of Negroes in the Knights of Labor." *J Neg Hist,* XXXVII (1952), 248-276.

12 LESTER, J. C. and D. L. WILSON. *The Ku Klux Klan: Its Origin, Growth, and Disbandment.* Nashville, 1905.

13 LEWINSON, Paul. *Race, Class, and Party: A History of Negro Suffrage and White Politics in the South. London, 1932.†*

14 MC WHINEY, H. Grady and Francis B. SIMKINS. "The Ghostly Legend of the Ku Klux Klan." *Neg Hist Bull,* XIV (1951), 109-112.

15 MATISON, Sumner E. "The Labor Movement and the Negro during Reconstruction." *J Neg Hist,* XXXIII (1948), 426-468.

16 PEIRCE, Paul S. *The Freedmen's Bureau: A Chapter in the History of Reconstruction.* Iowa City, 1904.

17 RANDEL, William P. *The Ku Klux Klan: A Century of Infamy.* Philadelphia, 1965.

18 RICHARDSON, Joe M. *The Negro in the Reconstruction of Florida, 1865-1877.* Tallahassee, 1965.

19 SCHEINER, Seth M. *Negro Mecca: A History of the Negro in New York City, 1865-1920.* New York, 1965.

20 SHAPIRO, Herbert. "The Ku Klux Klan during Reconstruction: The South Carolina Episode." *J Neg Hist,* XLIX (1964), 34-55

21 SINGLETARY, Otis A. *Negro Militia and Reconstruction.* Austin, Tex., 1957.

22 SMITH, Sanuel D. *The Negro in Congress, 1870-1901.* Chapel Hill, 1940.

23 SPROAT, John G. "Blueprint for Radical Reconstruction." *J S Hist,* XXIII (1957), 25-44. (On the military employment of Negroes.)

24 TAYLOR, Alrutheus A. *The Negro in South Carolina during the Reconstruction.* Washington D.C., 1924.

25 TAYLOR, Alrutheus A. *The Negro in Tennessee, 1865-1880.* Washington D.C., 1941.

26 TAYLOR, Alrutheus A. *The Negro in the Reconstruction of Virginia.* Washington, D.C., 1926.

1 WHARTON, Vernon L. *The Negro in Mississippi, 1865-1890.* Chapel Hill, 1947. (A pioneer revisionist study, of great importance.)†

2 WILLIAMSON, Joel. *After Slavery: The Negro in South Carolina during Reconstruction, 1861-1877.* Chapel Hill, 1965. (One of the most skillful and perceptive of recent monographs.)

3 WILSON, Theodore B. *The Black Codes of the South.* University, Ala., 1965.

4 WOODWARD, C. Vann. *The Strange Career of Jim Crow.* 2d ed. New York, 1966. (The basic account of hardening patterns of segregation.)†

5 WYNES, Charles E. *Race Relations in Virginia, 1870-1902.* Charlottesville, 1961.

See also **14**.8, **14**.9, **14**.10, **14**.11, **18**.12, **19**.1, **19**.2.

XXIII. Constitutional Issues During Reconstruction

6 BICKEL, Alexander M. "The Original Understanding and the Segregation Decision." *Har Law Rev,* LXIX (1955), 1-65. (The basic monograph on the attitudes of the framers of the Fourteenth Amendment toward segregation.)

7 BOUDIN, Louis B. "Truth and Fiction about the Fourteenth Amendment." *N Y Univ Law Rev,* XVI (1938), 19-82.

8 COX, LaWanda and John H. COX. "Negro Suffrage and Republican Politics: The Problem of Motivation in Reconstruction Historiography." *J S Hist,* XXXIII (1967), 303-330. (An inquiry into the motives behind the Fifteenth Amendment.)

9 EUBANK, Sever L. "The McCardle Case: A Challenge to Radical Reconstruction." *J Miss Hist,* XVIII (1956), 111-127.

10 FAIRMAN, Charles. "Does the Fourteenth Amendment Incorporate the Bill of Rights?" *Stanford Law Rev,* II (1949), 5-139.

11 FLACK, Horace E. *The Adoption of the Fourteenth Amendment.* Baltimore, 1908.

12 FRANK, John P. and Robert MUNRO. "The Original Understanding of 'Equal Protection of the Laws.'" *Col Law Rev,* L (1950), 131-169.

13 FRANKLIN, John H. "Jim Crow Goes to School: The Genesis of Legal Segregation in Southern Schools." *S Atl Q,* LVIII (1959), 225-235.

14 GILLETTE, William. *The Right to Vote: Politics and the Passage of the Fifteenth Amendment.* Baltimore, 1965. (The standard monograph.)

15 GRAHAM, Howard J. "The 'Conspiracy Theory' of the Fourteenth Amendment." *Yale Law Rev,* XLVII (1938), 371-403; XLVIII (1938), 171-194.

16 GRAHAM, Howard J. "The Early Antislavery Backgrounds of the Fourteenth Amendment." *Wisc Law Rev,* (1950), 479-507, and 610-661.

17 GRAHAM, Howard J. "The Fourteenth Amendment and School Segregation." *Buffalo Law Rev,* III (1953), 1-24.

18 HYMAN, Harold M. *Era of the Oath.* Philadelphia, 1954.

19 JAMES, Joseph B. *The Framing of the Fourteenth Amendment.* Urbana, 1956. (The standard account.)

1 KELLY, Alfred H. "The Congressional Controversy over School Segregation, 1867-1875." *Am Hist Rev,* LXIV (1956), 537-563.

2 KELLY, Alfred H. "The Fourteenth Amendment Reconsidered: The Segregation Question." *Mich Law Rev,* LIV (1956), 1049-1086.

3 KLAUS, Samuel, ed. *The Milligan Case.* New York, 1929. (Includes all the basic documents.)

4 KUTLER, Stanley I. "Ex Parte McCardle: Judicial Impotency?" *Am Hist Rev,* LXXII (1967), 835-851.

5 KUTLER, Stanley I. "Reconstruction and the Supreme Court: The Numbers Game Reconsidered." *J S Hist,* XXXII (1966), 42-58.

6 MC LAUGHLIN, Andrew C. "The Court, the Corporation, and Conkling." *Am Hist Rev,* XLVI (1940), 45-63. (Attacks "conspiracy theory" of Fourteenth Amendment.)

7 MATHEWS, John M. *Legislative and Judicial History of the Fifteenth Amendment.* Baltimore, 1909.

8 MAYERS, Lewis. "The Habeas Corpus Act of 1867: The Supreme Court as Legal Historian." *Univ of Chicago Law Rev,* XXXIII (1965), 31-59.

9 NICHOLS, Roy F. "United States vs. Jefferson Davis, 1865-1869." *Am Hist Rev,* XXXI (1926), 266-284.

10 RUSSELL, James F. S. "The Railroads in the 'Conspiracy Theory' of the Fourteenth Amendment." *Miss Val Hist Rev,* XLI (1955), 601-622.

11 SWINNEY, Everette. "Enforcing the Fifteenth Amendment." *J S Hist,* XXVIII (1962), 202-218.

12 TEN BROEK, Jacobus. *The Antislavery Origins of the Fourteenth Amendment.* Berkeley, 1951.†

See also **9**.3, **11**.1, **11**.3, **11**.4, **13**.8, **21**.1, **22**.25, **23**.11, **26**.3, **34**.9, **34**.10, **37**.3.

XXIV. Postwar Diplomacy

13 ARMSTRONG, William M. *E. L. Godkin and American Foreign Policy, 1865-1900.* New York, 1957. (Views of the editor of the influential *Nation.)*

14 BAILEY, Thomas A. "Why the United States Purchased Alaska." *Pac Hist Rev,* III (1934), 39-49.

15 BAXTER, James P., III. "The British High Commissioners at Washington in 1871." *Proc Mass Hist Soc,* LXV (1932-1936), 334-357.

16 BLUMBERG, Arnold. "George Bancroft, France, and the Vatican: Some Aspects of American, French, and Vatican Diplomacy, 1866-1870." *Cath Hist Rev,* L (1965), 475-493.

17 BROWN, Thomas M. *Irish American Nationalism, 1870-1890.* Philadelphia, 1966.†

18 CALLAHAN, James M. *American Foreign Policy in Mexican Relations.* New York, 1932.

19 CLARK, R. C. "The Diplomatic Mission of Sir John Rose, 1871." *Pac NW Hist Q,* XXVII (1936), 227-242.

1 DOZER, Donald M. "Anti-Expansionism during the Johnson Administration." *Pac Hist Rev,* XII (1943), 253-276.

2 DUNNING, William A. "Paying for Alaska: Some Unfamiliar Incidents in the Process," in Dunning's *Truth in History.* New York, 1937, pp. 118-133.

3 FARRAR, Victor. *The Annexation of Russian America to the United States.* Washington D.C., 1937.

4 GLUEK, Alvin C., Jr. *Minnesota and the Manifest Destiny of the Canadian Northwest.* Toronto, 1965.

5 GOLDER, Frank A. "The Purchase of Alaska." *Am Hist Rev,* XXV (1920), 411-425.

6 KEENLEYSIDE, Hugh L. and Gerald S. BROWN. *Canada and the United States.* New York, 1952.

7 KOHT, Halvdan. "The Origins of Seward's Plan to Purchase the Danish West Indies." *Am Hist Rev,* L (1945), 762-767.

8 LOGAN, Rayford W. *The Diplomatic Relations of the United States with Haiti, 1776-1891.* Chapel Hill, 1941.

9 LUTHIN, Reinhard H. "The Sale of Alaska." *Slavic and E European Rev,* XVI (1937), 168-182.

10 MAZOUR, Anatole G. "The Prelude to Russia's Departure from America." *Pac Hist Rev,* X (1941), 311-319.

11 MILLER, Hunter. "Russian Opinion on the Cession of Alaska." *Am Hist Rev,* XLVIII (1943), 521-531.

12 MOORE, John Bassett. *History and Digest of the International Arbitrations to Which the United States Has Been a Party.* 6 vols. Washington, D.C., 1898. (Includes much on the settlement of Anglo-American differences.)

13 PERKINS, Dexter. *The Monroe Doctrine, 1867-1907.* Baltimore, 1937. (The standard work.)

14 RIPPY, James Fred. *The United States and Mexico.* New York, 1926.

15 SHERWOOD, Morgan B. *Exploration of Alaska, 1865-1900.* New Haven, 1965.

16 SHIPPEE, Lester B. *Canadian-American Relations, 1849-1874.* New Haven, 1939. (The most thorough and authoritative treatment.)

17 SMITH, Goldwin. *The Treaty of Washington, 1871: A Study in Imperial History.* Ithaca, 1941.

18 SMITH, Joe Patterson. *The Republican Expansionists of the Early Reconstruction Era.* Chicago, 1933.

19 TANSILL, Charles C. *America and the Fight for Irish Freedom.* New York, 1957.

20 TANSILL, Charles C. *The Purchase of the Danish West Indies.* Baltimore, 1932.

21 TANSILL, Charles C. *The United States and Santo Domingo, 1798-1873.* Baltimore, 1938. (A full, scholarly, and impartial study.)

22 WARDEN, Donald F. "Drang Nach Norden: The United States and the Riel Rebellion." *Miss Val Hist Rev,* XXXIX (1953), 693-712.

23 WARNER, Donald F. *The Idea of Continental Union: Agitation for the Annexation of Canada to the United States, 1849-1893.* Lexington, Ky., 1960.

See also **5**.10, **10**.8, **13**.1, **13**.2, **13**.3, **19**.16, **26**.4, **27**.3, **27**.4, **31**.4, **31**.5, **31**.6, **31**.7, **31**.8.

XXV. Politics of the Grant Administrations

1 BARCLAY, Thomas S. *The Liberal Republican Movement in Missouri. 1865-1871.* Columbia, Mo., 1926.

2 CALLOW, Alexander B. *The Tweed Ring.* New York, 1966.

3 CRAWFORD, Jay B. *The Credit Mobilier of America.* Boston, 1880.

4 DOWNEY, Matthew T. "Horace Greeley and the Politicians: The Liberal Republican Convention of 1872." *J Am Hist,* LIII (1967), 727-750.

5 FAIRMAN, Charles "Mr. Justice Bradley's Appointment to the Supreme Court and the Legal Tender Cases." *Har Law Rev,* LIV (1941), 977-1034, 1128-1155.

6 FISH, Carl R. *The Civil Service and the Patronage.* Cambridge, Mass., 1904.

7 GREEN, Fletcher M. "Origins of the Credit Mobilier of America." *Miss Val Hist Rev,* XLVI (1959), 238-251.

8 HAYNES, Frederick E. *Third Party Movements since the Civil War.* Iowa City, 1916.

9 HOOGENBOOM, Ari A. *Outlawing the Spoils: A History of the Civil Service Reform Movement, 1865-1883.* Urbana, 1961.

10 HOUSE, Albert V. "The Speakership Contest of 1875: Democratic Response to Power." *J Am Hist,* LII (1965), 252-274.

11 KLOTSCHE, J. Martin. "The Star Route Cases." *Miss Val Hist Rev,* XXII (1935), 406-418.

12 MC PHERSON, James M. "Abolitionists and the Civil Rights Act of 1875." *J Am Hist,* LII (1965), 493-510.

13 MC PHERSON, James M. "Grant or Greeley: The Abolitionist Dilemma in the Election of 1872." *Am Hist Rev,* LXXI (1965), 43-61.

14 MANDELBAUM, Seymour J. *Boss Tweed's New York.* New York, 1965.†

15 RATNER, Sidney. "Was the Supreme Court Packed by President Grant?" *Pol Sci Q,* L (1935), 343-358.

16 RAWLEY, James A. "The General Amnesty Act of 1872: A Note." *Miss Val Hist Rev, XLVII (1960), 480-484.*

17 RIDDLEBERGER, Patrick W. "The Break in the Republican Ranks: Liberals vs. Stalwarts in the Election of 1872." *J Neg Hist,* XLIV (1959), 136-157.

18 RIDDLEBERGER, Patrick W. "The Radicals' Abandonment of the Negro during Reconstruction." *J Neg Hist,* XLV (1960), 88-102.

19 ROSS, Earle D. *The Liberal Republican Movement.* New York, 1919. (Still the standard account.)

20 ROTHMAN, David J. *Politics and Power: The United States Senate, 1869-1901.* Cambridge, Mass., 1966.

21 WYATT-BROWN, Bertram. "The Civil Rights Act of 1875." *W Pol Q,* XVIII (1965), 763-775.

See also **5**.10, **5**.15, **7**.1, **7**.2, **7**.3, **8**.10, **8**.11, **8**.12, **13**.9, **15**.5, **15**.10, **15**.16, **18**.3, **18**.4, **18**.5, **27**.6, **29**.10, **30**.5, **30**.6, **30**.7, **30**.8, **32**.1, **32**.2, **32**.3, **34**.6, **34**.7, **34**.8, **35**.9, **35**.10, **37**.1, **37**.2.

XXVI. The End of Reconstruction: The Election of 1876-1877

1 BRUCE, Robert V. *1877: Year of Violence.* Indianapolis, 1959. (Excellent on the social and economic background of the disputed election.)

2 DIPPRE, Harold C. "Corruption and the Disputed Election Vote of Oregon in the 1876 Election." *Ore Hist Q,* LXVII (1966), 257-272.

3 DUNNING, William A. "The Undoing of Reconstruction." *Atl Mo,* LXXXVIII (1901), 437-449.

4 HAWORTH, Paul L. *The Hayes-Tilden Disputed Presidential Election of 1876.* (Cleveland, 1906. (Long the standard account, though now somewhat outmoded; valuable for political detail.)

5 HESSELTINE, William B. "Economic Factors in the Abandonment of Reconstruction." *Miss Val Hist Rev,* XXII (1935), 191-210. (A seminal article, of great importance.)

6 ROSKE, Ralph J. "Visiting Statesmen' in Louisiana, 1876." *Mid-Am,* XXXIII (1951), 89-102.

7 STERNSTEIN, Jerome L., ed. "The Sickles Memorandum: Another Look at the Hayes-Tilden Election-Night Conspiracy." *J S Hist,* XXXII (1966), 342-357.

8 THOMPSON, E. Bruce. "The Bristow Presidential Boom of 1876." *Miss Val Hist Rev,* XXXII (1945), 3-30.

9 TUNNELL, T.B., Jr. "The Negro, the Republican Party, and the Election of 1876 in Louisiana." *La Hist,* VII (1966), 101-116.

10 WALLACE, D. D. "The Question of the Withdrawal of the Democratic Presidential Electors in South Carolina in 1876." *J S Hist,* VIII (1942), 374-385.

11 WOODWARD, C. Vann. *Reunion and Reaction: The Compromise of 1877 and the End of Reconstruction.* Boston, 1951. (A basic revisionist work, which explores economic forces working behind the political facade.)†

See also **10**.8, **13**.1, **13**.2, **13**.3, **26**.4, **27**.3, **27**.4, **31**.4, **31**.5, **31**.6, **31**.7, **31**.8.

NOTES

INDEX

A–B

INDEX

INDEX

INDEX

INDEX

INDEX

INDEX

W–Z